The HEART *of a* HEART WARRIOR

Anna Marie Jaworski

Megan Torres.

The HEART *of a* HEART WARRIOR

Congenital Heart Defect Stories of Hope

Anna Marie Jaworski
Megan Tones

Baby Hearts Press
Temple, Texas

Published by:

Baby Hearts Press, LLC

3910 Sierra Blanca Blvd.

Temple, TX 76502-1662 U.S.A.

First Printing 2023

"Michael's Poem" reprinted with permission from The Mended Hearts, Inc.

Excerpt from *In a Heartbeat* reprinted by permission from Kimberly Russell. *In a Heartbeat* was published by iUniverse in 2006.

"Overworld" Reprinted with permission from Megan Tones. "Overworld" was first published in *Masques*, edited by Gillian Polack and Scott Hopkins (2009, CSFG Publishing).

Excerpt from *From Vulnerable to Victorious* reprinted by permission from Tori Joy Geiger. *From Vulnerable to Victorious* was published by Tori Joy Geiger, LLC in 2021.

Excerpt from *The Hearts of a Girl* reprinted by permission from Jessica Carmel. *The Hearts of a Girl* was published by Morgan James Publishing in 2016.

Library of Congress Cataloguing-in-Publication Data Jaworski, Anna Marie

The Heart of a Heart Warrior / by Anna Marie Jaworski and Megan Tones

1. Congenital heart disease in adults I. Title

2. Heart–Diseases

3. Children–Diseases

Library of Congress Control Number: 2023933336

Publisher's Cataloging-in -Publication Data

Names: Jaworski, Anna Marie, editor. | Tones, Megan, editor.

Title: The heart of a heart warrior : congenital heart defect stories of hope / Anna Marie Jaworski and Megan Tones.

Description: Temple, TX : Baby Hearts Press, 2023. | Includes index. | Includes 72 photos. | Summary: A collection of personal narratives from people impacted by congenital heart defects.

Identifiers: LCCN 2023933336 | ISBN 9780965250801 (pbk.) | ISBN 9780965250870 (ebook)

Subjects: LCSH: Chronically ill – Biography. | Congenital heart disease – Patients – Biography. | Heart diseases – Patients – Biography. | Pediatric cardiology.
| BISAC: BIOGRAPHY & AUTOBIOGRAPHY / Medical. | HEALTH & FITNESS / Diseases & Conditions / Heart. | SELF-HELP / Motivational & Inspirational.

Warning–Disclaimer

This book is not intended to be medical advice. Medical information described in this book is solely for illustrative purposes.

This book is not intended to be a text for medical treatment of children with congenital heart defects (CHDs). Parents should consult with medical personnel whenever they feel compelled, regardless of what is written in this book.

The areas of pediatric cardiology and congenital heart disease are ever changing. This book has reported some adults' past experiences. For a more in-depth analysis of treatments of CHDs, the reader is encouraged to visit the library or conduct an online search in relevant medical journals.

Every effort has been made to ensure this book is as accurate as possible; however, there may be mistakes, both typographically and in content. Consequently, this book should not be used to define medical treatment for any child or adult. Many of these stories are written from adult heart warriors' memories of what happened to them many years ago or what their parents remember. These people may have been in shock when given certain medical information, thus there may be inaccuracies. These contributors have taken great pains to write with as much accuracy as possible.

The purpose of this book is to inspire others. The authors and Baby Hearts Press shall have neither liability nor responsibility to any person or entity with respect to any loss or damage caused, or alleged to be caused, directly or indirectly by the information contained in this book.

Loving Supporters

Thank you to our Kickstarter Donors!

Allison Holmes

Amy and Eric Bjorkman
in honor of Emma Beth

Amy M. Le, CEO of
Quill Hawk Publishing

Ana "Annie" Ulchak

Angel Santiago of Cedarwood
Financial Partners

Anonymous (3)

The Atherton Family

Ayden Ahola and Family

Belén Blanton, Founder/CEO
of Fundación Estrellita de Belén

Bellamy-Friedmans in honor of the
Jaworski family

Bob & Theresa Daigneault

Brandon Lane Phillips, M.D.

Brenda and Cara Vignaroli
in honor of Jessica

Brian, Dana & Evan Henning

Carol Hulsey in honor of Kim Russell

The Castiglia Family in honor of
Daniella Rose

Charlie and Bonnie Gamez

Chris Padgett

Christina Kunze in honor of Eddie

Dr. Corinne Smorra

DanJoAnn Gorsich

Dawn and Wayne Martin
in memory of Travis

Debi and Steve Sigrest

Deena Barber in honor of
all ACHD patients

Derrick, Bethany, and Sophie Tilbury

Edward Bove, MD

Ernest Co

Goodman and Sons

Grace Pensiero

Grandma Judy

Grant Martin

Greg McHenry

Gwen Fosse

Heather in memory of Johnathan E.
Caldwell and Laurea M. Ardito

Helen Goldstein in memory
of Stacey and in honor of Jill

Hilary Uhr

Holly Pham

In honor of Andrew Helton

In honor of Ryan Kier

In memory of Daniel Cross and
in honor of Peyton Bledsoe

Jackie Renfrow in memory of
Jimmy and Crissy

Loving Supporters

Thank you to our Kickstarter Donors!

Jennifer Schoondyke in memory of Kari Elizabeth

Jesus Loves You

Jian Wang

Jill Sorensen in honor of Jeni Busta

Jody K Jaynes in honor of Michelle DeRoo

Joey, Ashley, and Rowan in honor of Hope Jaworski

Joshua and Deborah Frost

Judi and Andy Harmon

Julie Roush Butler in honor of Hayes Charles McKinney

Julie Vuong

Kealey Martinez

Kim and Tom Russell

Kris Gupta, MD

Lauren Elizabeth

Len N. Wallace

Lita Daniel

Lonnie Gruner

Lorraine McDaniels in honor of Nicole

Margaret Hopson in memory of Julie Ann Hopson

Marina Lohri

Mary Kay Klein in memory of Karen and James McNulty

Marylisa Diorio in honor of Matthew Detterline

Meagan Cross

Melissa and Paul Friedman

Melissa Geiser

Michael and Leora Liben in memory of Liel

Michelle DeRoo

Michelle Steltzer in memory of Gregory J. Romenesko

Mike Dandridge

Monica A. Mossey

Nancy and Karl Jensen in memory of Jessica Marie

Nicholle Bilodeau

Pam Davis in honor of Marcus

The Redferns

Ric Stapp

Rita Scoggins

Rob Smith and Dot Cannon

Robin Naeger

Roseann and Ben Bischoff in honor of David Franco

Roseann Franco in memory of David

Saveeda Shaikh

Loving Supporters

Thank you to our Kickstarter Donors!

Sheila and Wayne Allred in honor of Olivia Ann Williams

Sheri and Steve Turner in memory of Thomas

Shirley Anderson in honor of Michelle DeRoo

Sophie Diaz

Stephanie Gregory

The Sullivan Family in honor of Travis Martin

Summer Lawlis

Tabitha Moe

Terrie Russell in honor of Kimberly Russell

Texas E. Reardon IV

Tracy Livecchi

The Valentine Family

Vermont Heart Heroes

Zuzu Miranda

I am a Miracle Child

by Becca Atherton

I am a miracle child
Struggling the first months of my life
Given a 13% chance of survival to the age
of five Today I am 17
I am a miracle child

Life-saving battle scars adorn my body
Changing my shirt, I see the bright pink
scar running down my chest
Always a reminder of my yearning for life
I am a miracle child

Fear is part of me
I am afraid when my heart skips a beat
I fear being in the hospital
Alone . . .

In pain . . .
I cry at the very thought
I fear dying
I am a miracle child

I know I am not like most
Valuing life
I celebrate the morning
I appreciate those who love me
And know
Every day truly is a gift
I am a miracle child

Being a miracle child
Is . . . Frightening,
Is . . . Celebrating,
Is . . . Accepting,
Is . . . Appreciating,
Is . . . My life
I am a miracle child

Dedication

Megan and I would like to dedicate this book to all the wonderful people who contributed to the book and whose legacy are the words and stories they have left behind so that we might better understand them. We especially lovingly dedicate this book in memory of Karen Klein McNulty, Julie Kerr, Becca Atherton, David Franco, and Travis Martin, contributors we lost before the book was published, and to all who have loved them. We also dedicate this book to the entire congenital heart disease community. It is an honor to be part of this special group.

I also dedicate this book to my own heart warrior, to my heart- healthy son, and to my husband, who is everything to me. AMJ

I would like to dedicate this book to those who listened to me and helped save my life over the years - my mum and dad, who must have felt like they were raising an alien at times, my brothers, husband, and extended family, and of course, all the medical professionals. MJT

Table of Contents

FOREWORD

My name is Dr. Corinne Smorra. I am a licensed clinical social worker specializing in working with those impacted by congenital heart disease (CHD). I was born with truncus arteriosus. I have spent every day of my life as a CHD patient, but the last several years working to help those who have been affected by this condition. As a counselor, I work to provide the support, understanding, and most appropriate psychosocial interventions for people born with heart disease–an invisible birth defect that affects them far beyond the confines of their hearts.

My friend Belén Blanton, who you will meet in this book, introduced me to Anna. She knew Anna Jaworski through her podcast, *Heart to Heart with Anna*, which has been running since 2013. Anna not only has a child with CHD, but has also edited the first two books in this series, *The Heart of a Mother,* and *The Heart of a Father.*

Anna and I first "met" on the phone. There was an electric charge between us as we shared our mutual passion of wanting to contribute to the benefit of the CHD community. Anna and Megan have spent the last four years working on this book of essays written by those who have been born with CHD. They have done an amazing job compiling and editing the authors' stories about their experiences and challenges, and optimism about their lives.

When I think about how to describe these stories, the one word that reverberates the most is resilience. As you read each piece, I can honestly say no matter what the outcome, or obstacle each heart warrior faces, the resilience they show will jump off the page and grab at your heartstrings. Kimberly Russell, who responds to someone who tells her, "Oh, it's too bad you did not have the experience of having a child," with "Well, it is too bad you did not have the experience of adopting."

I appreciated Megan Tones, who learned how to sew because she had difficulty getting clothes to complement her body alignment. Then there's the essay by Jeni Busta–who as a child was bullied ferociously. When you read her essay, you'll see how faith, love, and perseverance have allowed her to quell negativity which might have consumed her. People pushing their physical limits beyond the expectations their doctors shared with them intrigued me. Reading about heart warriors achieving milestones and their successes made me happy. Lastly, you will read stories about those who inherently knew there was something going on with their health. They believed they needed to push further and keep digging for answers, challenging different doctors until they found a solution together.

The reason I write the foreword for this book is that psychosocial research on adults with CHD is approximately 10 years behind what we see for children who have CHD. This book will help provide some answers and support while the research can catch up. In the meantime, if CHD is impacting your life in some form, this book can serve as an immediate support for you or a loved one. The fact is, many adults with CHD encounter anxiety and/or depression. A book like this one can normalize the feelings, as well as provide some confidence in oneself. I like to say to my clients facing uncertainty, "It's smart to plan for obstacles but necessary to hope and plan for the best, as well. We do live each day with an underlying concern, but we want to make sure we grasp those opportunities for the future."

Dr. Corinne Smorra, DSW, MSW, LCSW

Chief Clinical Officer (CCO), Heart and Mind Counseling LLC

Adjunct Associate Professor, Western New Mexico University, School of Social Work

Contributing Faculty, Walden University, Barbara Solomon School of Social Work

PREFACE

Welcome to the book we wish someone would have given us many years ago. Our dream with this book is to provide a resource to let others in the congenital heart defect (CHD) community know they are not alone. Who are we? The editors are a parent of an adult with a CHD (Anna) and a heart warrior (Megan). We came to know each other thanks to Facebook. We have known each other since January 2015, but it feels as though we have always been part of each other's lives, although 8,261 miles separate us, with me being in Temple, Texas and Megan being in Brisbane, Australia.

Living with CHDs in the 21st century is better than it was when most of the contributors to this book were born. When they were born, there was no Internet, more babies were born every year than there were adults alive with CHDs, and medicine was more of a trust-me-I'm-the-doctor type of practice, rather than one based on family-centered care.

My heart warrior was still a child, and I didn't even know Megan when the idea for this book was conceived. While a handful of adults with CHDs wrote for my two other anthologies (*The Heart of a Mother* and *The Heart of a Father*), the idea of having a book entirely written by heart warriors was still a dream, especially since my wish was for my own child to be a contributor.

It has taken us years to gather essays, work with the contributors, and refine our vision for the book, but it has finally happened. As scary as it is to be the parent of a child with a CHD or an adult with a CHD, these are miraculous times we live in. The diagnostic tests available, drugs and supportive devices [such as implantable cardiac defibrillators (ICDs), left-ventricular assist devices (LVADs), and even implantable loop recorders] make the management of CHDs something that is less scary and more successful. They have refined the surgical procedures to help those born with CHD over years, which now sometimes include the use of robotics, 3-D printing, and even stem cells to help our heart warriors live their best lives. These types of technologies are game changers. It truly is an exciting time for us to be alive to witness history in the making.

That is what makes this book so valuable and so unique. Many of the people who have written for this book were some of the early pioneers. These children had parents who refused to give up on them and who decided that a potential future was better than no future at all. Parents gave permission to surgeons, cardiologists, and other medical professionals to do what had to be done in order to save their children's lives. They put their trust in the medical system, and the field of pediatric cardiology blossomed. Today, there are often multiple procedures available to help medical teams treat their patients, and there are enough results from previous cases to give them an idea of the potential outcome.

Sadly, there is a downside to being a pioneer. Bullying, confusion, misinformation, and uncertainty were part of everyday life for many of our heart warriors and their families. Many heart warriors were told they were "fixed" after their first surgery and, for some, they would lead happy, healthy lives, until an unexpected event would land them in the emergency room. Depression, anxiety, and post-traumatic stress are all conditions that many heart warriors (and their family members) experience because of the circumstances involved with such uncertain futures. Myriad hospitalizations and procedures, and even conflicting solutions from professionals, depending on when and where care was administered, contributed to challenges with mental health. This book is needed because of the shared experiences so many heart warriors understand. People need to know they are not crazy, they are not misinformed, and they are not alone.

This book is for all the people in the CHD community who believe that their lives, or the lives of their children, siblings, grandchildren, or friends, matter. They had lives worth saving, despite the trials and tribulations. Here is a book for anyone who has dealt with a broken heart but who chose to look at the whole person instead of just a damaged organ. This book is for the believers, the dreamers, and the fighters. This book is for all heart warriors and their families. Thank you for the sacrifices you have made. May the stories in this book make your hearts a little lighter, and may you realize, if you didn't know this already, that you belong to a very special subset of the world.

Anna Marie Jaworski

ACKNOWLEDGMENTS

This publication took over four years to go from concept to actual book. First, we need to acknowledge and thank every person who contributed to this book. We wrote, edited, and revised essays repeatedly. We have grown closer to these amazing people and their stories inspire us. Since you can easily see the names of each of the contributors in the Table of Contents and throughout the book, we won't list each of them here, too. However, I would like to acknowledge a few family members who helped us with contributions, especially after a heart warrior passed away. Special thanks to Chris Atherton, Roseann Franco, Roseann Bishop, Mary Kay Klein, Arlyn Kerr, and Dawn Martin. We really appreciate you helping us to make sure the contributions were the legacy your loved ones deserved.

When talking to some friends about who could write the Foreword to this book, Belén Blanton immediately knew who would be perfect. Thank you, Belén, for introducing me to Dr. Corinne Smorra. Thank you, Dr. Smorra, for helping others understand the purpose and significance of this book.

I would like to thank members of Facebook who responded to polls. We would like to thank our beta readers, especially Joe Flowers, Lowri Smith, Beth Greenaway, Julie Valladares, Helen Simpson, Kimmie Salvage, Sasha Elizabeth O'Donnell and her daughter Odette, Daphne Davis-Patrick, Deena Barber, Sheri Turner, and Cora and Valerie Guerin. Feedback from the congenital heart defect community is so important! Thank you especially to Jane Hunt, Debbie Gilmore, Rita Scoggins, Amy M. Le, and Jenny Muscatell—all of you are always there with helpful advice and an encouraging word.

There are always people behind the scenes who are instrumental. Brenda Vignaroli was our webmaster extraordinaire! She did so much to help me in the early stages and until Lauren Elizabeth took the reins from her. Lauren did a wonderful job of revamping the website just in time for the launch of Baby Hearts Press as a hybrid publisher. Janet Scherer and her daughter Stephanie have also provided encouragement and support. Thanks to Monica Mossey, the spreadsheet queen, we had a list of people who wanted to be part of the book and their contact information.

Many of you know this book is the third in the *The Heart of a …* series. I'm indebted to Lisa Colvil for working with me for hours to come up with an agreed-upon design. There was no photo or art that seemed perfectly able to depict a "heart warrior," so Lisa and I decided that putting all the words commonly used by the CHD community in a heart was the way to go. Omer Farooq took our idea and gave it life. This is our special Kickstarter-only cover.

Our goal with this book was to have one place where adult heart warriors could share important aspects of their lives with the world to stand as a testament to the resilience of the human body and mind. The pages that follow are not the stories in their rawest form. Instead, Megan Tones and I worked with each author to help them craft their stories. Amy M. Le even added a helping hand in the developmental editing phase and gave several contributors her helpful insight. I know that other family members, friends, and writing buddies also helped in this process. I'm sorry not to have the names of all those people to give credit where credit is due, but if you're reading this and you were one of those helpers, thank you.

Megan Tones met with me regularly to edit, work on formatting the book, help with communicating with our contributors and so much more. Having a co-editor who actually was a heart warrior was something I felt was necessary to give this book the tone it needed. I knew Megan understood each and every story with every fiber of her being. As a heart mom, I could appreciate the stories, but Megan lived many of those stories, thoughts, and experiences. Also helping with the editing, formatting, and design work with the book was heart warrior and contributor, Lauren Elizabeth. Thank you for helping us finally get the advanced reader copies of the book ready for distribution and getting the book ready for publication.

Our husbands were instrumental because they sacrificed many hours that we could have spent with them in order to let us work on this book. Frank

Jaworski and Matthew Tones have never wavered in their support and love for us during this book project. Frank also always fed me and kept me hydrated. Thank you to both of our significant others for keeping us sane during the tenure of this project!

Although it may seem unconventional, I think we also need to give a thank you to our furry children who were literally by our sides during so much of the process. My miniature Schnauzer, Missy, often insisted on sitting on my lap or on my feet when I first started this book. After she passed away, Buck and Chloe were almost always on the pillow by my desk, on my feet, or somewhere in my office while I worked. It is because of them I would get up to take breaks and I never felt lonely while working on the book.

Belle often slept on the top of the lounge chair behind me, snoring loudly for a toy fox terrier, while her younger sister Pandora curled up in the sun. Together, they were my office ladies, although they were often joined by their brothers, Kratos and Brutus. Sadly, Brutus and Belle are no longer with me; however, their passing enabled us to welcome Coco and Bella. Alas, Kratos now has three younger sisters and often looks a bit frazzled as he curls up on my lap. (Co-editer, Megan Tones)

Finally, I believe there were many angels on our shoulders while we worked on this book, and I would like to acknowledge that. Sadly, we have lost too many friends in the CHD community far sooner than we would have liked. I need to acknowledge my mother, who also passed away in 2018. In her last days, she dealt with A-Fib and I learned even more about treatments that many of our heart warriors must endure, but it's thanks to my mother's Texas-sized heart that I learned how to love others from a young age. If I had to sum up this book in a word, that's the word I'd choose—"love."

INTRODUCTION

In the year 2000, I was 17 and on the cusp of adulthood. As my classmates bought cars, went on dates, and planned their gap years or daydreamed about sharing houses and university, I just looked forward to the next day when I could lie on the lounge and watch music videos. Even though I dropped every class I could without affecting my capacity to graduate, I still nodded off in class and had trouble focusing. I just managed to pass even though I had top marks in primary school and junior high. Aware that I had a heart condition, the teachers gave me a pass. My English teacher even told me I could go to sleep while the rest of the class watched Macbeth. Unbeknownst to me and everyone else, I was living with untreated heart failure. I didn't know anybody else with a congenital heart defect (CHD), and my only involvement in the CHD world was when I went to my paediatric cardiologist every two years, who always told my parents and me I was fine.

At my graduation, the high school gave out several awards. The Class of 2000 sat in the gymnasium with their families as they announced various achievements—top marks for core subjects like English, Maths, and Sciences, and several sports and community awards. Then came "Achiever of the Year." My name was called. I walked up to the bright stage with the duxes and athletes, where a local member of parliament smiled and handed me a certificate with both hands. She whispered, "I understand it takes over an hour for you to get to school." Perplexed, I nodded.

As the speeches went on, I wondered why I had received the award. It had been a rough year for my family with several personal problems, which affected my studies to where I received special consideration. My family had moved two years ago, and I wanted to stay at my old school, even if it meant commuting across town by train. Still, I knew of several other students facing personal difficulties and a long commute. Why was I singled out? I felt self-conscious standing up there holding an award that I received simply for staying in school.

My cardiology team finally discovered my heart failure in my mid-20s, and I found out that not only was I not cured, but that I needed another surgery. This crisis prompted me to google CHD, and I found what I had sorely been missing in life—education about CHD and a supportive community. Words can't express how validating and empowering it was to discover that world. I met many wonderful people from across the globe who'd had similar experiences to me. All of them helped me so much just by listening and sharing. I have stayed in contact with the community since then, and I feel like it would take an entire lifetime to pay it forward, but I do what I can!

When Anna approached me about this book in 2018, I had already known her for a few years. In 2015, I was a guest on her podcast, and before long, I started working as a scriptwriter for Heart to Heart with Anna. *We would get together with our dogs on Skype or a Facebook call, and brainstorm together to write captivating bios and questions for her many guests over the years. I knew she had edited two books written by heart mothers and heart fathers, so, I was very excited when she raised the idea of editing a book written by adults with CHD. I saw a wonderful opportunity to create a resource. I thought back to when I was an exhausted teenager wondering how on earth I would be an adult—and what a difference a book like this might have made.*

As a person with CHD myself, words like "hope" and "inspiration" make me cringe a little, as I think back to the award I received at my graduation and how it made me feel. It was like people telling me I was brave and strong for going through this or that procedure, when I didn't feel I was doing anything other than what I had to do. However, I truly believe that this book conveys a sense of hope and inspiration to people living with CHD and their families. Not because the authors have CHD and get up and live their lives like everyone else, but because of the creativity and tenacity they display to be heard, prove others wrong, and do the best they can, even if sometimes they had to go about life a slightly different way than they'd planned.

I hope you will read these diverse essays and see yourself and your loved ones represented, and maybe even imagine a future you didn't think would be possible. Anna and I organised the book into 10 different chapters, each representing a different theme. You may start from the beginning or read whichever chapter/s you like the sound of. There is also an index in the back to help you find topics of interest to you. When I write, the text will be in italics to differentiate my writing from Anna's. You'll notice that my spelling might be a bit different from Anna's, since she's from Texas and I'm from a little place called Brisbane, Australia. We felt it was important that we, and all the contributors, share their words and spelling as they would in their homeland.

Megan Tones

Survival

In the late 1990s a popular reality television program, *Survivor*, took the world by storm. The first of these programs, called *Expedition: Robinson*, was a Swedish television show. The format for the program involved a group of contestants who gathered, usually in a remote, exotic location, to compete for a cash prize. People were ousted one by one until there was a sole survivor. It was a wildly popular program around the world and especially in the United States in 2000.

Survival for our heart warriors isn't so entertaining. Survival often means enduring open-heart surgery. It frequently means besting the complications that often accompany having had one's chest opened while surgeons perform life-saving procedures. Survival means having gone through so many diagnostic tests that Beads of Courage could stretch from one city to the next. Survival often comes at a price—but it also comes with bragging rights.

In the four chapters that open this book, you'll read about survival in its rawest form. You'll meet heart warriors and read about what growing up meant for them. You'll learn about how their heart defect does, or does NOT, define them. You might be amazed at how some heart warriors are active with their CHDs, and you'll discover clever ways they've learned how to navigate their lives to focus on their successes instead of their challenges. Finally, you'll learn about heart warriors around the globe and you'll witness how CHDs affect people of every nation, every socioeconomic status, and every race in very similar ways. The fact that the contributors to these essays have survived is remarkable in and of itself. It is because they survived and lived to tell about it that we even have this book at all.

CHAPTER 1

GROWING UP WITH CONGENITAL HEART DEFECTS

When Anna first put out the call for essays on heart warriors' experiences in overcoming obstacles, I was eager to get started on my essay. My head was so full of ideas from things that had happened to me as a child or an adult. Do I write about my flashes of memory as a five-year-old in hospital—being fed pieces of a lemonade ice block as I emerge from surgery or stalking around the shiny, disinfected jungle dressed in a leopard costume my mother made me? In my imaginary play, I was always strong and powerful, a stark contrast to how I felt in life. Or do I write about the open-heart surgery I had when I was 10, that I still don't really understand? About the growing sense of unease as the atrial flutters got worse? My nervous friends? Or the nurse who read me Paul Jennings books on the day of my surgery?

What changed between five and 10 years of age was a growing sense of how I differed from others. From the stories and poems you will read in this chapter, you will see that difference runs through all of them. Whether it is being self-conscious about a new scar as a teen, as in Laura Ryan's 'It Takes a Child,' or facing stares and questions about a personal and traumatic health battle, as Dajah Scrivner describes in her poem, aptly titled 'I Am Different.' Tyler Šajdák and I write about other complications associated with CHD, vocal cord paralysis, and scoliosis respectively, and how they affected us socially.

Fortunately, from my time at school, I cannot recall any bullying incidents related to my heart. My fellow students were very kind in that respect. When I was in hospital at ten, there was another boy in my ward. I think his name might have been Gavin, but I know for a fact his cats' names were Ben and Rambo (I always had a better memory for animal names than people). He told me a story one day, "I was in the playground one time and this other kid started making fun of me because of my pacemaker. So I kicked him in the nuts and he fell off the jungle gym."

When I look back at my time growing up, I see how fortunate I was that my classmates were so kind to me. Even as a teenager, when I wore a back brace for my scoliosis, I can count the number of nasty comments I received on one hand. Unfortunately, Jeni Busta did not have the same experience, as she detailed the horrific bullying she endured for her heart condition in 'A Soul Unbroken.' However, throughout these stories, there is a sense of acceptance, resilience, and growth. This is especially clear in Michael McKelvey's poem. Our authors in this chapter range from their early 20s to their early 50s, yet there are common threads through them. I hope you enjoy the essays and poems about growing up with congenital heart defects.

It Takes a Child

by Laura Ryan

In May 1986, I had my second heart surgery. I was 16 years old and had a fresh "zipper" scar. "Mom, can't we go somewhere else for our vacation this year?" I asked my mother as she was packing her suitcase.

"Laura! You love Lancaster!" she exclaimed.

"But, Mom, we always go to the water slides in Lancaster. It's time we did something different," I said.

"I don't know what's gotten into you," my mother said. "This has always been your favorite place on earth."

I did not want anyone to see my scar. Swimming without a shirt covering my bathing suit (and my scar) was out of the question. Why didn't my mother understand that?

It was the first time in my life I was self-conscious about my body. I never had a "zipper" before. My first heart surgery was done when I was six weeks old. It was a closed-heart surgery done through my side. By the age of 16, the scar was old and faded. Now I had a "zipper" scar running down the center of my chest. It was fresh, only three months old, and still red and bumpy.

As we approached the slides, the smell of chlorine was in the air. People were applying sunscreen and a comfortable feeling of summer wafted over me, only to be quickly replaced by dread. There were new owners.

New owners with new rules. 'No shirts allowed on the slides' was printed in large red letters and I felt my heart sink.

"Let's go!" said my younger sister. I refused to go. I wanted to go, but there was no way I was going to take my shirt off.

I watched Michele dash to the slides, squealing with delight. I burst into tears. "Why are you crying?" Dad exclaimed. "You love it here!"

I turned away. "What's wrong with her?" Dad asked Mom.

Why didn't they understand? Couldn't they see this ugly red scar on my chest? Didn't they understand I didn't want people staring at me?

"Laura, you're being ridiculous!" Dad said. He threw up his hands, shaking his head, and walked away from me.

Mom quietly said, "Laura, you are strong. Your scar is proof of how tough you are."

"You just don't understand!" I sobbed and hid my face in my hands.

Suddenly, I heard a shout. "Look, Mom! Look!" said a very excited little boy as another family entered the picnic area. Two little boys about five and seven years old were dragging their mom to a table near us. The older of the two started stripping off his clothes. "Come on, Mom!" he shouted. "It's getting crowded! Let's go!"

The younger boy slowly walked over to the picnic bench and sat down. He started crying. "Come on!" the older brother cajoled. He tried to help his younger brother take off his shirt, but the little boy pulled away from him.

Mom started talking to the little boy's mom. "My son just had heart surgery," the other mom whispered.

Mom nodded and said, "I understand. What kind of heart defect does he have?" The two mothers started talking a mile a minute. By this time, I had stopped crying and was staring at the little boy.

'He's too young to be self-conscious about his scar' I thought.

"Yes, my daughter has also had open-heart surgery," Mom was telling the other mother.

The boy stopped crying and stared at me. I made a funny face at him. I crossed my eyes.

"Oh, yes. It was the longest day of my life," said one mother.

I stuck my tongue out to the side and crossed my eyes again. The boy copied me.

'We are being silly,' I thought. 'We can both have a lot of fun.'

"And he was born without an earlobe," the boy's mom continued. "He's had all kinds of reconstructive surgeries on his ear and they still aren't finished!"

I started thinking about it. I wore glasses, and they did not bother me. I had a scar on my side, and that didn't bother me. It was then that something changed in me. I walked over to the boy and said, "Hi! I'm Laura. Would you like some chips?"

We bit into the salty potato chips and gobbled them down while our mothers brought us each a Coke. We talked, sipped our cold drinks and laughed at some other kids' silly antics near the slide. After a few minutes, I took off my shirt. The boy smiled and took off his shirt. "Looking good!" I said and gave him a thumb up sign. When he smiled back at me, it lit up his eyes. Simultaneously, we said, "Let's go!" as we grabbed the water slide mats and started walking hand-in-hand to the kiddie slide.

"Just a minute!" the boy's mother exclaimed.

"Laura, you'll burn to a crisp!" Mom admonished as she tossed me a tube of sunscreen.

We spent the rest of the afternoon going up and down the Jack and Jill kiddie slide. We got water up our noses and had to go back to get more sunscreen before the day was done. Chlorine burned our eyes, but we didn't care.

Thanks to a young boy, I started enjoying myself and got over being self-conscience about my zipper. All I had to do was to look beyond myself to see the situation more clearly. Sometimes it takes a child.

Laura Ryan was born April 9, 1970 in Brooklyn, NY and raised in Queens, NY. She was born a "blue baby" with a single left ventricle and congenitally corrected transposition of the great vessels. Laura has two biological sons and has been married since 1995. She loves all animals and has cats, dogs, turtles, and frogs. A little-known fact: Laura collects salt and pepper shakers!

A Soul Unbroken

by Jeni Busta

As the door closed, I walked to the corner of the bathroom and slumped into a fetal position. With my arms wrapped around my knees, I bowed my head, closed my eyes and felt the tears sliding down my cheeks. "God," I whispered. "Please take my life. I don't want to live anymore!"

I had just been washing my hands in the bathroom when I heard the school's fire alarm bell ringing. Some girls started taunting me, saying, "Why don't you just stay here and let the building burn and fall on you, Jeni? You're gonna die young anyway." It was 1991, but those voices still haunt me to this day.

At the beginning of each school year starting in preschool, my mother was invited to present a fun and educational lesson about the differences between my heart and a normal heart. Mom unrolled two big posters—one with a normal heart and the other with a hypoplastic left heart syndrome heart. Passing out stethoscopes to my peers, Mom said, "Here, let's listen to each other's hearts!" While my classmates took turns listening to each other's hearts, Mom continued, "Jeni has a special heart. Doctors had to do surgery, and she has a special machine in her tummy that helps her heart beat better." As if on cue, I would then lift my shirt, showing my scar. Mom would then hold up an x-ray, showing my chest and my pacemaker in my stomach. "Sometimes Jeni gets tired, but she can still run and play with you."

While most of the kids learned from Mom's presentation, some classmates were unkind. In 1989, in preschool, some time after Mom's presentation, a little boy punched me in the stomach because he thought it would be cool to see my insides spill out.

The next year, I was walking outside before lunch, and a little boy ran up to me. I stopped walking to look at him. "I'm gonna bring a gun to school tomorrow," he said. Stunned, I started crying. "If you tell your family, I'll go to your house and shoot them, too!" For two decades, I

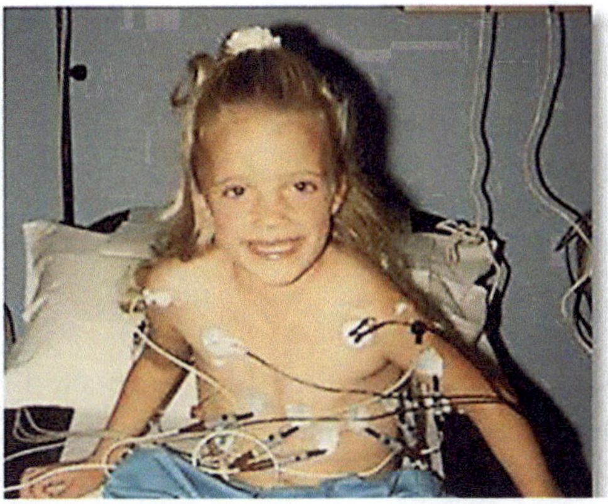

had recurring nightmares where this same kid (as a grown-up) would come to our house and kill my family members as I hid behind the couch. When the shooting was over, I would see them lying dead on the floor with a bullet through their heads.

A common occurrence happened when I walked around the schoolyard during physical education, as I was unable to run laps for very long. My schoolmates then would run up behind me to shove me to the ground. While laughing at me and running off, they yelled, "You can't be our friends, Jeni, since you can't run as fast as we can!"

Even in my lowest places, I knew God was with me throughout it all. My scar was nothing to be ashamed of but rather something of beauty. It was God that knitted my heart (Ps.139:13-14) exactly as He wanted it, and He never makes mistakes. My bullying experiences continue to make me a compassionate counselor for others living with CHD.

At six years old, all I wanted was to stop living. Little did I know that three years later, I would be at a heart camp on an island surrounded by kids who were just like me. They had scars on their chests, medicines to take, and the understanding of what it's like to think that every day could be their last. If God took me home when I was six years old, I never would have known what it was like to grow up with people who understood what it's like to live every day with a heart defect like the people I met at Camp Del Corazon.

I wish I could say that being bullied is all in the past, as I am now a woman in my mid-thirties. I feel I am expected to have a college degree, a successful career, or raise a family. However, because of the limitations of my condition, I have had to determine what my life goals are. Some people have been very critical regarding what they think I should do with my life without considering the limitations of my heart defect. This has taught me that seeking the approval of others is like chasing after the wind. (Ecclesiastes 2:11) It is futile.

If God had taken me home when I asked Him to, I would never have met Nick Busta.

Nick came along when I least expected it. I caught his attention with a Bible verse (Philippians 4:13—I can do all things through Him who gives me strength.) We were 14 years old when we met online in Random AOL Chatroom #25. My profile said, "I was born with half a heart (HLHS)." Nick said, "Oh, that's really sweet, you're waiting for your other half." Nick soon learned the truth about my heart defect.

Nick and I were practically inseparable, even though we lived 300 miles apart for the first four years of our relationship. We talked nightly for hours on the phone with calling cards. We emailed love letters to each other. Then it was finally time to meet in person. "Mom, I fell in love with a boy online and I want to meet him. Will you please take me to meet him?"

God gave me Nick to help mend my emotional scars from being bullied. Nick believes I am beautiful regardless of what my classmates used to say. My husband Nick is my rock, support, and cheerleader who keeps me thriving. On July 14th, 2007, I married my other half and best friend.

God has not only blessed me with the most amazing husband I could ever hope or ask for, He has also blessed me with an incredibly loving and Christian family. They have all been there to encourage and strengthen me in my faith. Whenever the memories of my being bullied are brought to mind, I am reminded of my favorite Bible passage. James 1:2-4 which reads, "Consider it all joy, my brethren, when you encounter various trials, knowing that the testing of your faith produces endurance. And let endurance have its perfect result, so that you may be perfect and complete, lacking in nothing (New American Standard Bible, 1995)." This is God's promise to me that no matter what I was going through,

He used my pain to help me grow in endurance and strength. I know that whatever trial I face, I am assured that God has His purpose for me in mind. He has shown me that His plan and purpose was much bigger than that which I was able to comprehend at six years of age. I hope that one day, when I finally meet my Creator, I will be completely healed of my emotional scars and that God will make my heart whole.

Jeni Busta was born on June 25, 1985 at UCLA Medical Center with hypoplastic left heart syndrome (HLHS), or an underdeveloped left side of the heart. In essence, she was born with only half of a working heart. She grew up in Camarillo, California, with her close-knit family. She became involved in the CHD community at a young age and attended Camp del Corazon, a camp for children with congenital heart disease, for nine years. In the summer of 2007, she married her sweet husband Nick and is now a happy housewife who still advocates in the CHD community. Her advocacy revolves around her faith in Jesus Christ and sharing her story to give hope to others.

Picasso

by Megan Tones

My face grew warmer with each passing second as I stood touching my toes in the nurse's office, feeling the eyes of the nurse, my teacher and my classmates burning into my back, blood rushing to my face. I watched the nurse's feet pace back and forth behind me. Even when I closed my eyes, I could hear the *CLOP CLOP* of her high-heeled shoes.

'This is taking too long. Something's wrong.'

I didn't find out how wrong until a few weeks later in the specialist's office. He sat opposite my mother and me; the light reflecting off his spectacles, making him look like a mad scientist in a horror movie.

"How could I have scoliosis and not know, with all the chest x-rays I've had?"

"Defects of the heart and spine often go together," he said bluntly.

He turned on a light to view the x-ray on the screen. I saw a slight bend in the thoracic spine, a cross marked above it with a number–13. 'Little, lucky 13.'

Over the next three years, that little number grew to 23, to 31. The crosses on my x-rays seemed to get bigger too, reminding me that my body had gotten something else wrong.

"Megan, do you know any other girls at school with a brace?" The specialist looked at me with his shiny, shiny eyes.

What kind of question is that? I paused as my mind did the gymnastics to find an answer that would avoid me getting a brace.

He was trying to break the news to me gently, like that old "not so fast" joke. All the sergeants who have a mother step forward. "Not so fast, Sergeant Jones."

We drove home from that appointment in silence with me hypnotised by the white dotted line in the centre of the road, an endless, straight vertebrae.

By the next week, we were in another waiting room. I studied the goldfish glittering under the harsh tank lighting, listening to the endless bubbling of the filter. I was almost in my own world when someone kicked my shoe.

"Megan?" I nodded. "C'mon. Let's go." Another doctor trying to be my pal. Great.

Within a short time, I was wearing a tight body stocking strapped to a rack, which was like a hospital bed, but with soft plastic slats instead of a mattress. I stretched my body to lengthen and straighten my spine.

"We're going to make a body cast for your brace." He began wrapping a wet plaster bandage around my chest. I winced, expecting the bandage to be cold and slimy like seaweed in the ocean. It was warm, and I breathed out as far as I could, feeling the brace push against me. Was this what the next three years would be like?

After what felt like an hour, the cast was dry and the doctor cut it off. What a relief, I thought as I washed the plaster off my body and got changed again.

A couple of weeks later, my brace was ready. It was made from hard, inflexible white plastic with dense foam on the inside, and reminded me of the Stormtrooper armour from Star Wars.

The doctor opened the brace from the back and wrapped it around me. "Just do it up loosely while you get used to it." He adjusted the Velcro straps, and the brace closed like a set of jaws, jerking me right and left. I tried to breathe deeply and felt an itch on my belly, now out of reach.

I looked at my reflection in the consult room. Aside from my heart condition, I had received the four horsemen of adolescent humiliation: braces, headgear, acne, and now the mother of all of them—a back brace.

I tried to pull my jeans over my instantly wider hips. The waistband yielded, but there was no hope for the zipper. Next was a camisole. It revealed my brace in all its glory, especially on the left side, where the brace dug into my left armpit. With only track pants and t-shirts fitting me, I saw a silver lining.

"How about we go shopping?" My mother asked.

The teen girl section at the local department store was filled with midriff tops and tiny shorts, like an army of invisible mean girls. 'Thanks a lot, Spice Girls.'

"None of these will work."

"These clothes aren't really your kind of thing, anyway." Mum said. She was right, but the problem was I couldn't wear them.

In the ladies' section, I had more luck.

"I don't want to wear stretch jeans. Fat old people wear those."

"Nobody will know." Mum said. "Just try them and see what you think."

I was surprised in the change room. The jeans went over my brace and the zipper closed easily. They looked just like my old jeans.

"Those look good." Mum said. "With a t-shirt, you wouldn't even know you were wearing a brace."

Those jeans and a t-shirt became my uniform for that winter, but come summer, there was another problem.

"All the dresses that hide my brace are from the old lady section." I said. "They look like church clothes."

"I have an idea." Mum said.

My mother had sewed since she was a little girl and made clothes for me when I was younger. At first, I thought I was too old to wear home-made clothes, but my only other option was looking like a 15-year-old granny.

"Look." She showed me some patterns of fitted dresses. "I could make this in a fabric you like and adjust it so your brace doesn't stick out."

"I don't know . . . "

I hadn't been to a fabric store since I was little. I thought back to when the rolls of fabric were taller than me, and I would run around the store like I was in a technicolour forest with the scent of wool and fresh cotton, looking for buttons with cute animals on them. Now, I was on a mission. We left with a pretty blue floral cotton.

I tried on the dress when it was finished, and what a transformation! For the first time since I started wearing my brace, I felt better about myself instead of worse. The brace faded away under the fabric, leaving only curves that were meant to be there.

As a child, I sewed toys but quickly became frustrated with sewing clothes in home economics classes at school. Newly motivated by how good a well-fitting dress could make me feel and my disdain for department store clothing, I started sewing my own clothes by the time I was 16. I made a long purple maxi dress I wore until it was full of holes.

When I was 17, my specialist gave me some good news. "You've stopped growing. You can discard your brace now."

I threw my brace in a metal bin in the backyard. Then the bin mysteriously caught fire. Looking back, I wished I had kept the brace and turned it into some kind of art project, but the melted mess expressed my feelings.

Unfortunately, the end of brace wearing did not mean the end of scoliosis. My spine still curves and rotates to the right, and on a bad day, it feels like a flame licking up and down the length of my back, burning my nerves in its wake. One shoulder rotates forward, my ribs bow out front and back on opposite sides, and I have had to go to a Schroth therapist to manage the pain.

My mother took me to a professional dressmaker about three years ago. I was shocked by how different the measurements of the left and right side of my body are. To help with fitting, my dressmaker drafted separate left and right pattern pieces for my body. When I cut out a pattern, it looks like it's designed to fit one of Picasso's figures, but somehow it all comes together.

When I put one of my dresses on, I still have that amazing feeling of being transformed by a piece of clothing that was made to fit me.

Megan Tones was born in Brisbane, Australia, in 1983. She was suspected of having a heart problem at six days of age when her mother noticed her gaining weight despite difficulty feeding. At four months of age, she had a pulmonary artery banding and received an official diagnosis of ventricular septal defect (VSD) at two years of age. More surgeries followed, including a VSD repair at age five, a right ventricular outflow tract reconstruction at age 10, and a mitral valve repair as an adult.

Today, she lives with a husband (Matthew), four dogs, heart failure, and the occasional arrhythmia. She works as a researcher at Queensland University of Technology, and likes to travel, attend movies and the theatre (not operating), and sew, paint, and write. You can reach her at meganjtones@gmail.com.

Michael's Poem

by Michael McKelvey

Hearts woven, hearts been broken,

Deep down my chest, I've been sliced wide open.

Born not knowing, scars clearly showing,

The pain and discomfort, but I am slowly growing.
The power of a man to understand what's in his hand,
He's dumbfounded in the light but still sticks to the plan.
Unfolded the truth, untold to be shown,
Scars lie even deeper than what he's ever known.
Wicked limits hassled and strangled the life from within.
Fighting every breath for forgiveness of sin.
Painted melodies of gluttony and sorrow,
He often feels like his life is being borrowed.
He fights and fights just wanting to be heard,
His heart sings, but without any words.
His heart aches for just one day to be healthy,
But even he knows money can't save him, no matter how wealthy.
That's why he remains smiling, and is happy as can be,
Even though his scars will never leave.

Editor's Note: This poem was initially published on the Mended Little Hearts website. We thank them for permission to reprint it here.

Michael McKelvey was born on January 15, 1992, in Sharon, Pennsylvania, with double outlet right ventricle (DORV), ventricular septal defect (VSD), and total anomalous pulmonary venous return (TAPVR). He has had four open-heart surgeries. He loves basketball and is a huge Kobe Bryant fan. Michael believes that if we are kind to one another, we can help change the world.

I am Different

by Dajah Scrivner

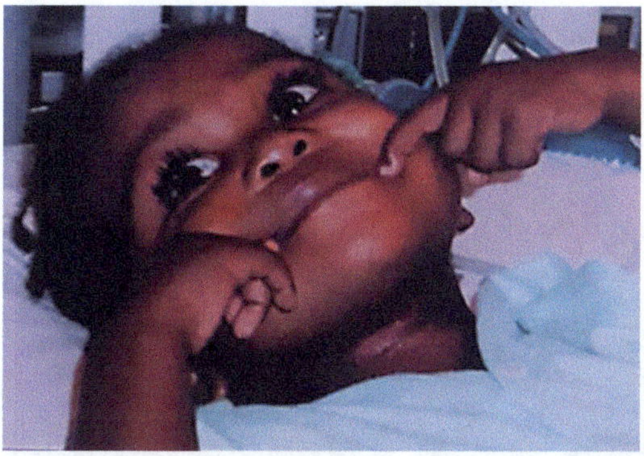

I was only two years old on December 13, 2004
Sirens blasted as I laid on the floor
Paramedics bring me back following a cardiac arrest
To be forever marked as "different"
Looking at my scar in the mirror, I knew I was different.
People staring at me and asking, "What happened?"
I just stare at them and start to cry
Because I am Different
Asking my gym teacher, "Can I sit out? I might pass out."
Or just taking medication every day from a young age.
Going to doctor appointments just to see if everything is ok.
Because I am Different
Every year on December 13th, I cry and people don't know why.
Not every kid can tell what happened to them on a specific day.
Sometimes I wonder why
I am Different

Dajah Scrivner was born July 6, 2002 with double outlet right ventricle (DORV). Her hometown is Clarksville, Tennessee. Dajah loves to work out, and she has an eight-year-old Rottweiler named Ruby (after her birthstone).

Voiceless

by Tyler Šajdák

Growing up without a voice is an incredibly difficult thing to do. It forces you to figure out ways to cope with other people that most others never have to think about. From constantly being asked to repeat yourself to only speaking up when you think it's necessary, it gives you the incredible opportunity to become a superb listener. That was my life for my first 14 years on earth.

Although I was always involved in playing sports as a kid, the shortness of breath and lack of verbal communication made things tough, especially as I grew and the fields that I played on got larger. This became especially pronounced when I started playing high school baseball the summer after 8th grade. In Little League and rec leagues, I grew up playing shortstop or pitcher in most baseball games I played. But, when I got to the first practice for the freshman baseball team, I quickly realized there were much better athletes that also played shortstop and pitched. I also realized that we didn't have anyone who wanted to play catcher. My path of least resistance to playing every game was to sit behind the plate.

I have always loved the strategy of baseball and playing catcher is just like a second coach on the field, calling pitches, giving signals to the rest of the team and calling out where the throw should go since I'm the one who has the best view of the whole field. Despite having never played catcher before in my life, I quickly fell in love with the position. During one of our practices, my coach was hitting ground balls and fly balls to the rest of the fielders, and I was attempting to call out where the throws had to go and if they should be cut off by the infielders. I was trying my hardest to get my voice out to them, but the fielders were struggling to hear what I was saying. My coach noticed this, and I made the comment that my voice will be better able to handle shouting instructions to the fielders next season, but until then, this is what I'm working with. The coach asked how I knew it would be better next season, and to explain this, we have to go back in time.

The previous fall, my father, brothers, our foreign exchange student, and I were out in our yard playing football. The ball ended up on the ground and we all went to go pick it up. We ended up in a pile on the ground. We all thought we were unharmed after this event, but a few days later, my dad's voice went hoarse as he was talking to my mom. He ended up making an appointment to see an ear, nose, and throat doctor in Des Moines, Iowa, the closest specialist to us.

My dad got to talking with the team there and brought me and my history up. My parents were told that I could have the nerve that attaches to my vocal cord fixed, but it would require a rather invasive surgery and it would leave me with a large scar across my throat. But, as he was talking about me and my voice, the doctor told my dad he could fix it. My dad asked how he would do it. The doctor replied that it would be a laparoscopic procedure. The doctor would go in through my left armpit area with three small rods, one with a camera and two with the tools, and take a nerve from my throat that was used for swallowing and attach it to my vocal cord, inject some collagen into my vocal cord since it was weak because it hadn't moved in 13 years, and I would have a voice when I woke up from surgery. We were all confused why we hadn't heard about this procedure before, since this is a common issue among congenital heart defect patients. The doctor told us he had just started doing it this way.

The August between 8th grade and freshman year, after baseball season was over, I had the procedure done. I woke up and everyone was able to hear me for the first time in my life. My parents were in tears when they heard. I called my maternal grandparents on our way home from the hospital and they were in tears as we talked. A few weeks before I had my surgery, my paternal grandfather had a stroke. He wasn't able to communicate very well because he lost most of his motor function after the stroke.

When we got back home after my surgery, my uncle went to the hospital to visit my grandpa and he called me up, knowing that I had my surgery and that one of my grandpa's biggest frustrations was his difficulty hearing me. My uncle put me on speakerphone and brought the phone close to my grandpa and I just talked to him. For the first time in my life, my grandpa could hear me without all the barriers that we had previously. Tears streamed down his face. That was the last conversation that I had with my grandpa as he would pass about a week later. I don't remember what I said in that conversation, but I will never forget that feeling that I had and all the barriers falling just like that.

When I walked into school a few weeks later, all my friends at school were happy to hear me and my baseball coach, who was also the history teacher, told me he was looking forward to hearing my thoughts in class and being able to call out instructions to my teammates on the diamond next season.

Even almost 15 years later, I still struggle with some effects of not having a voice for the first 14 years of my life. Sometimes I talk too fast. I still listen before I speak most of the time. I don't always enunciate clearly enough for people. But gaining a voice has opened up doors I never thought would open. I was able to be on the radio during high school. I participated in healthy (and unhealthy) debates in school. I was able to give speeches in class without worrying if the teacher sitting in the back of the room would be able to hear me. Despite all the drawbacks that I had growing up, I don't know what I would do now if I didn't have a great family, friends, and the ability to speak for myself.

Tyler Šajdák is a 29-year-old with hypoplastic left heart syndrome. He holds a bachelor's degree in Political Science and currently works for the University of Pittsburgh. Tyler enjoys watching and playing sports, often going to Pittsburgh Pirates games and playing in local slow-pitch softball leagues. He can also be found watching movies and television shows in his spare time.

CHAPTER 2

HOW MY CHD DEFINES ME

When I decided to put together a book of essays by adults with congenital heart defects, I asked my heart warrior to contribute. I had tentatively named the book *The Heart of a Heart Warrior* and I asked for an essay.

"I'm not a heart warrior. I'm not a survivor or a thriver, either."

"Write about that," I said.

I said that not all "heart warriors" perceived themselves as such and that in the 27 years I'd been a member of the congenital heart defect community, those terms "heart warrior," "heart survivor," and "heart thriver" were fairly new. There were other people who felt the same way my heart warrior did, and they needed their views validated, as well.

With reluctance, my heart warrior wrote an essay, received feedback, revised it, and finally got it into a form that everyone was satisfied with. During the four years that we have been working on this book, my heart warrior has been going through a more important transition. My heart warrior was born Alexander and lived as a male for 27 years. In January 2022, Alex informed Frank and me he no longer identified as a male. Hope is the new name my transgender daughter prefers to go by. She doesn't want to be identified by her cardiac condition. She wants people to know her for who she is aside from her heart condition, but she's one of the lucky ones. Yes, she's had three open-heart surgeries, but she's been able to fully recover and she leads a full life, which includes full-time employment, living alone in an apartment, and a life full of friends, family, and activities.

Not everyone born with a heart defect is that lucky. Some people who are born with heart defects are not privileged enough to lead the life they wish they could. Low saturation levels handicap them, they have to adjust their schedules because of some drugs they must take, they're recovering from complications from some cardiac procedure, or they simply lack the energy to work full time. Sometimes people's hearts give out completely, forcing them to make some really tough decisions.

Should they opt for an assist device? Should they have another surgery or procedure? Do the risks outweigh the benefits? Should they opt to be put on the transplant list? For some people, their heart dictates their lives, whether or not they want it to.

One term I've learned from working on the *Bereaved But Still Me* podcast is 'post-traumatic growth' and it is a term that means growth from a traumatic experience. I believe I've experienced post-traumatic growth over the years by working with people in the CHD community. Some adults with CHDs also experience that kind of growth.

In this chapter, you'll meet my daughter, but you'll also meet two other heart warriors. Jason Crutchley had to make some of the hard decisions I alluded to earlier. He tells us how his heart defect has defined him. Christy Sillman, while not needing a heart transplant like Jason, has faced other trials in her life and, from some of those experiences, she has grown into a remarkable woman, mother, and nurse.

Not a Heart Warrior

by Hope Jaworski

I could be a warrior. But what does it mean? Why do some people consider themselves warriors and others don't? I'm not a heart warrior, but I have been a warrior in Dungeons and Dragons. So why one and not the other?

"Why are we stopping already?" Phil the barbarian asked. "There's still sunlight; we can keep going."

"Sure, but this way we get to sleep in a bed before reaching the forest," I pointed out.

"Boring," he grunted as he looked longingly toward the cursed forest, hand resting on his giant axe.

I searched my cloak for a pouch of money, tossing him one full of copper coins. "Here, go drink to your heart's content," I suggested, smirking as his eyes lit up. "We'll go buy some supplies and meet you at the inn later."

He headed off merrily, accompanied by Randy, our paladin, to make sure he didn't start a tavern brawl for the fun of it. The wizard, the cleric, and I went to the marketplace, spending our meager savings on what food and equipment we could afford for the upcoming journey.

"Just one last adventure," the wizard, Linda, sighed. "Then we can retire."

"Are you ready to live the rest of your life in peace?" I asked. "No more running around, finding monsters and fighting for your life?"

"Absolutely!" she nodded emphatically. "Someone else can take care of monsters, we've done our part."

"It's still kinda fun," I admitted as I examined a collection of daggers, wondering if I could justify buying one. "I might be at it for a while longer."

"Not me," she shook her head. Our team's cleric nodded in agreement with her.

"Well, more power to you. When you're living it up in the big city, I'll come visit you," I said, forking over a couple of gold coins for the enchanted blade I wanted.

Warriors have some agency in the matter. We get to have adventures and face danger on purpose. There's an end in sight, an option to let others take up the torch and carry on with your work. I've never felt that with my heart condition. It's always felt forced on me, and every part of dealing with it is just a burden. Not everybody's like that; we all see things differently and uniquely, and that's important to understand.

Another tree exploded as Linda hurled fireballs. The goblins ran away screaming, Phil giving chase. We let him go; he'd make his way back soon enough. The rest of us started putting out the fire before it could spread.

"How much more of this?" Randy asked. "There can't be that many more monsters in here."

I checked my bag. "Nah, there's more," I said.

He looked at me sternly. "You mean you need to loot more gold from them?"

"Someone's gotta pay the bills," I said as I examined a dropped sword, wondering if it would be worth carrying around to sell to someone. "Besides, we're making a big difference. How many travelers did they ambush and kill? We're making this place safer."

The burnt tree crashed to the ground behind us, continuing to smolder. Linda had moved on to another tree, trying to put it out before the fire got out of control.

"As soon as we've achieved our purpose, we should leave them be," Randy said firmly. "Violence only gets you so far."

I pocketed some more gold coins as I continued searching the bodies. To each their own, after all.

Warriors get something meaningful out of their work. Whether it's serving a higher purpose, helping others, or just putting food on the table, they can feel they've achieved something. That they're helping, or even just have the right intentions. Struggling with my heart defect isn't about gaining anything; it's just about living. It's survival, nothing more than that.

The sun was rising as we left the forest, dragging the troll king's body behind us. The villagers saw our approach and cheered as we entered the gate. I tossed some silver coins to them, grinning as they scooped them up eagerly.

"Thank you, brave adventurers!" the village chief approached us, beaming from ear to ear. "How can we ever repay you for this act of kindness?"

Feeling the weight of the solid gold crown in my bag, I waved away his offer. "Don't worry about a thing, sir," I said, shaking his hand. "We're just trying to make the world a safer place."

"Got any more of that good ale?" Phil asked.

Most of the village followed us back to the tavern for drinks and a party. The troll king's body was taken to be disposed of, though I'm sure the tusks and some other parts would be turned into trophies. We didn't need it anymore. A bigger reputation and some gold were enough. We celebrated until well past sundown, the entire village full of life after being freed from the monster's presence. We ate better than we had in weeks and slept soundly in comfortable beds. It was truly the best reward we could ask for.

At the end of the journey, a warrior revels in their victory. CHDers have such long roads to recovery, and not everybody sees an end to that journey. Even those of us that can rest and be at ease know that it'll happen again one day. There are some things in common to the life of a warrior, but to me, the differences stand out more. I'd make a fine warrior, especially in games, but I'm not a heart warrior. And that's okay. Everybody should look for what they're good at and then be the best version of themselves that they can be.

Hope Jaworski was born in Temple, Texas with a single ventricle heart in 1994. She lived as a male under the name Alexander for 27 years before realizing and accepting that she was a transgender woman. Hope enjoys writing, playing tabletop games with friends, and 3-D printing. She worked in healthcare for eight years.

How My CHD Defines Me

by Jason Crutchley

All of us are defined by what we are born with. For a person born with a congenital heart defect, that is certainly true, however it's how it defines us that makes us all different. In 1976, I was born with atrial septal defect, transposition of the great vessels, subaortic stenosis, and pulmonary atresia. My mother was told I wouldn't make it past my first hour. After several hours, she could take me home.

I continued to survive for another six weeks, when I had my first procedure called a pulmonary banding. Again, the odds were stacked against me and they expected me to only have three good years. At age six, I was the first child at UCLA to undergo the Fontan procedure—with a 2%

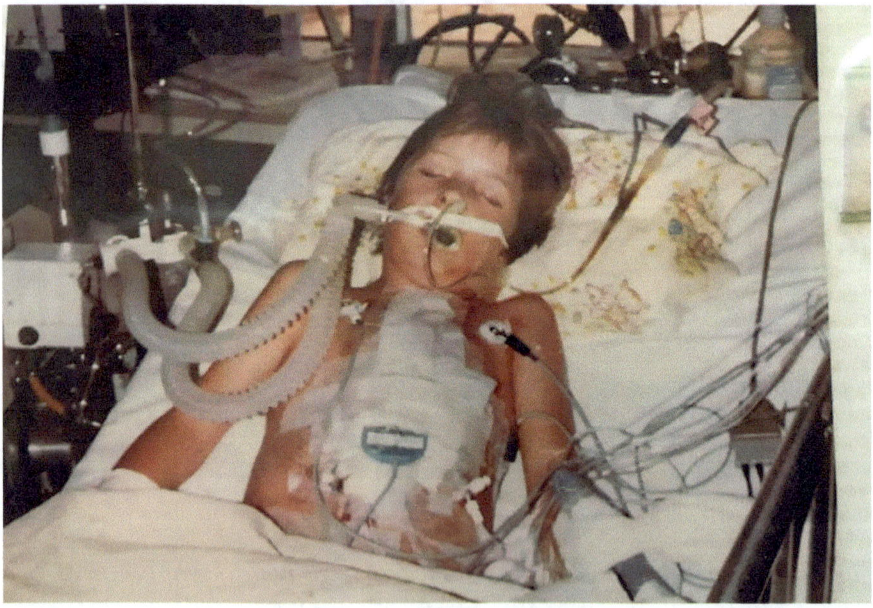

survival expectancy. Years later, I had several episodes of SVT in which cardioversion was the only treatment. At 21, I had a lateral-tunnel conversion revision of the Fontan. Three pacemaker surgeries had followed by the age of 23.

Because of all the help I received as a child, I knew my mission. My calling was to help others. I recall shortly after my Fontan surgery telling my mother I wanted to be a pediatric cardiologist and always thought I couldn't wait to get my license plates for my car, which would read IAMADOC. I later decided maybe I wanted to be a police officer, or firefighter, or even get into the military. However, because of my heart conditions, I realized this could never come to fruition.

In 2005, I recall watching the horrific devastation left behind by Hurricane Katrina. As I sat down to eat dinner with my family at our dinner table, I couldn't stop thinking of all of my fellow Americans who wouldn't be able to enjoy a hot meal on their dinner table with their families and my heart just sunk. I knew deep in my soul that I had to do something, but didn't know what or even how to help.

The following morning, the American Red Cross was raising money during a telethon for the victims of Hurricane Katrina. While being interviewed, the Red Cross worker asked for 250 volunteers who could immediately be deployed to the affected areas of Katrina to help. I knew at that exact moment that is how I could help. With no hesitation, I called the American Red Cross. After getting clearance from my cardiologist, and several grueling hours of training, I found myself on my way to help the victims of Hurricane Katrina as an American Red Cross Disaster Services Volunteer.

Finally, my chance to give back to others what I was given throughout my life, a fighting chance. My deployment brought me closer to what I had always wanted to achieve in this life. It brought me closer to new friends and a new family. The work was hard, tedious, and often overwhelming. Hours were long and the days never seemed to end. I would go to bed so exhausted from my day and wake up early the following morning, eager to get back to my job. After my 2-week deployment, I returned home grinning ear to ear knowing I made a difference in someone else's life.

I knew without a doubt, this is what I was supposed to do. I have since deployed to nearly every major disaster in the U.S., except for a few because of my health. Having fulfilled my goal of serving my country, I have helped thousands of others in their greatest time of need. I am defined by my CHD. Because of my congenital heart defects, I am defined to help others by offering my time, energy, and talents with just as many skilled and talented nurses, doctors, and surgeons have done with me.

Jason Crutchley currently resides in Chesterfield, VA but his hometown is Sacramento, California. Jason was born with an atrial septal defect, transposition of the great arteries, sub-aortic stenosis, and pulmonary atresia. He is a cancer survivor, stroke survivor, and heart and liver transplant recipient, thus effectively giving him two birthdays; 3/4/76 and 1/28/19. When he's not working, Jason's favorite activity is cruising on the open water.

Finding Myself Through Service to Others

by Christy Sillman, NP

"So, why do you want to work as a cardiovascular pediatric ICU nurse?" asked one of the panel interviewers as we began my most nerve-racking and life-changing job interview.

"I don't," I said with deadpanned confidence. Their jaws hit the floor.

"I don't want to work here. This is the place of my greatest anxiety, fears, and traumas, but I am *compelled* to work here. I have a passionate drive to work with children who have congenital heart disease, because I, too, have congenital heart disease."

A common debate in the adult congenital heart community centers around when we should disclose our congenital heart disease (CHD) to other people, especially at our place of work. Many people rightfully are concerned that it will make employers wary of hiring or promoting them. Other times, people worry that disclosure of their CHD will make them appear weak or incapable.

I have found that many adults with congenital heart disease (ACHD) either believed the judgments and severely depend on others despite being very capable, or they overcompensated for this judgment by being some of the most ambitious individuals I've known.

My complex CHD has drastically shaped who I am today, and it's difficult for me to privatize such an important part of my self-identity. However, for the first half of my life, I rarely talked about my CHD. I wasn't ashamed of it; I just didn't feel I needed it as part of my identity. Deep down, even when my pediatric cardiologist told me I was cured "because you turned 18 years old," I knew that this was never something that was going to go away. I had to incorporate my congenital heart disease within my self-identity.

I never thought I'd work in the medical field. I had always had my sights on Hollywood and a professional acting career. However, when my fourth open-heart surgery at 17 years old resulted in a paralyzed vocal cord and losing my stage and singing voice, I was forced to reevaluate my life. The messages from the universe all kept pointing me in one direction—nursing. It was unexpected but, ultimately, the best choice.

Then I applied for that job in the cardiovascular pediatric ICU. I don't even remember applying; it was almost as if I was guided to it from a higher power. I believe my honesty in the interview gave me that job and I began a wonderfully terrifying career as a pediatric cardiovascular critical care nurse.

I found it difficult at first to balance my two identities as nurse and congenital heart patient. I worried that when I shared my CHD with my patients and their families, I was instilling a false sense of hope through my lived testimony. My mom reminded me that there was never anything false about hope. Overall, my lived truth became my strength as I practiced with a personal level of empathy and compassion.

Despite my direct involvement with inpatient pediatric congenital heart care, I was still caring for myself under the false pretense that I was "cured" of my CHD and that I didn't really need cardiology care. I finally listened to my gut feeling that this was wrong and began seeking care, but wasn't sure where to go. I was too old for pediatric cardiology but felt too young to be with the older acquired heart disease patients in general cardiology.

It wasn't until I was pregnant with my son that I discovered the Adult Congenital Heart Association and the field of Adult Congenital Cardiology. I cried tears of joy as I read about these physicians who had undergone specialized training to care for adults who had previous congenital heart surgeries (many with outdated techniques) while learning about the long-term consequences of living our entire lives with abnormal hemodynamics and scar tissue within our hearts. I was fascinated with the research being done in this field, from both a medical perspective and a personal perspective. As the newest medical subspecialty in 30 years, adult congenital cardiology has a unique opportunity for discovery that feels endless. I began immersing myself in the field and patient advocacy organizations to try to find a place within the community.

As fate should have it, I was introduced to Dr. Susan Fernandes, the program director for the Adult Congenital Heart Program at Stanford, at a national conference. Dr. Fernandes's expertise, presentation, and passion for the care of ACHD patients immediately impressed me. I asked her advice on how to combine my passion for ACHD care with my career, and she recommended I apply for an upcoming nursing position with her program.

Dr. Fernandes recommended that I not speak about my CHD during the interview process and rely solely upon my professional experiences to exemplify my candidacy for the position. I found it impossible to keep hidden as each interviewer asked me why I wanted to work in the field of adult congenital cardiology and ultimately disclosed my truth. It is what makes me who I am and to hide it feels deceitful and wrong.

I've been the nurse coordinator for the Adult Congenital Heart Program at Stanford for nearly five years and I'm preparing to leave in just a few months to return to school and train as an acute care nurse practitioner. I'm uncertain of where I'll be practicing once done with school, but I know I will work in Adult Congenital Cardiology. I've found my calling and truly can't see myself doing anything else.

Throughout my career as a nurse, I have strived to remain mindful of how and when I disclose my CHD to my patients and their families. I have lived by the tenant that if it doesn't serve to strengthen the therapeutic relationship, bring about a higher sense of empathy, or provide relatability, then it isn't necessary to share. I never want it to be "about me" and maintain the focus of my interactions on my patients' lived experiences.

I've also struggled with comparisons. I've lost patients with similar diagnoses as myself. Patients struggle with fears and terrors that I can relate to. I have yet to undergo a major cardiac procedure since becoming a nurse, but I know it's in my future and I hope I can navigate the experience gracefully. The patients who have taught me the most about resilience live in peaceful acceptance of the natural fear associated with living with CHD.

In *Daring Greatly*, Dr. Brené Brown states, "Because true belonging only happens when we present our authentic, imperfect selves to the world, our sense of belonging can never be greater than our level of self-acceptance."

Through my career, I've learned to find a partnership with my CHD, and have found a level of self-acceptance that I never knew was possible. I am a nurse living with congenital heart disease, and I have found myself through helping my fellow CHD warriors.

Christy Sillman was born in September 1980, with tetralogy of Fallot with pulmonary atresia. Her hometown is Sacramento, California. She is married to Steve and they have a son named Noah. Christy is an adult congenital heart disease nurse practitioner.

CHAPTER 3

BEING ACTIVE WITH CHD

I never thought I would write the introduction to a book chapter about being active with a congenital heart defect, as I didn't even like sports video games (except for Mario Kart*), but here I am. At school, I dreaded physical education and sports days, as I felt like my heart defect was on show for the entire school. One time, I was so far behind the other kids in the race that the teacher fired the starting gun for the next race. Before I knew it, I was lapped by not one, but two groups of kids and I managed to lose two races at once! I still got a sticker, but I believe that incident started my hatred of competitive sports. Fortunately, in my old(er) age, I have learned that the best competitor is yourself and I now work towards improving my fitness.*

The first two essays are about finding new lifelong pathways to enjoy exercise and sports when complex CHD impedes your first choice. Lorrie Hill and Michael Hills (no relation) both had big dreams when they were young: Lorrie, of becoming a physical therapist, and Michael a hockey player.

Undeterred, Lorrie shifted her interest towards researching the malformed heart's response to exercise, and Michael found his passion for sports in baseball, watching hockey, and competitive curling, sports requiring both skill and endurance. Today, both Lorrie and Michael are studying towards careers in health and sports.

The other two essays are about exploring physical activity via other interests. Alicia Lynch, who has complex CHD, started experiencing arrhythmias just after finishing high school. Her symptoms pointed to a need for a Fontan revision, which was a shock for the young graduate. However, Alicia found that the surgery opened up new opportunities for her, as she joined a dance group at college and performed in several shows. The last essay is about a trip to Egypt I took with my husband shortly after I turned 30. While almost all the insurance companies felt I would be a liability, our tour guide believed in me and worked tirelessly to create the trip of a lifetime. While I was no Lara Croft, I was grateful to have the experience of climbing amongst such ancient monuments.

I hope you enjoy these essays, and that they encourage you to find new ways of being active that align with your goals and interests.

For the Love of Exercise

by Lorrie Hill

The icy, icy wind blew through my hair and my heart was pounding in my ears while flipping around in my chest as my friend and I ran in from recess on one of the few winter days Houston had that year. We had missed the five-minute warning bell and barely heard the "time to go in" bell. The third-grade teacher on duty, who was not aware of my heart condition, yelled, "Hurry up! Recess is OVER!" Afraid we would get in trouble, we decided running was the only option.

When I got back to the classroom, my teacher looked at me, then quickly told a student, "Lead the class into another classroom." While she tried not to panic at the "close-to-blueberry" shade of blue I was, she slowly hurried me to the school nurse's office. Sit, lay down, take some deep breaths, and cool down," said the obviously scared nurse. She helped me pull off the jacket I was now sweating buckets under. She knew I just needed time.

That day, I decided I hated active physical activity despite the fact I had loved trying dance, cheer, soccer, and basketball (my favorite) through the years. I was done!

For the rest of elementary and middle school, I was the artsy academic, really diving into the wonder of science. In eighth grade, I learned about high school athletic training. The program would give me an opportunity to learn basic anatomy and hands-on experience in treating and preventing athletic injuries. The "athletic" part made me leery; I knew it would not include any running, but I was nervous. Thus far, I had stuck to my conclusion that exercise was detestable. I was afraid that I could not physically or mentally do it.

The next time I was encouraged to exercise was a day after having my second open-heart surgery that summer. In a dazed state, over the beeping of machines in my cardiovascular intensive care unit (CVICU) room, I heard "Do you want to try to stand and move to a chair?" from a bubbly physical therapist (PT) that had just walked in. I just had heart surgery and I am extremely sore; of course I don't want to move, I thought. I knew I did not have a lot of say in the matter so, I obliged. "Swing your legs over and scoot to the very edge of the bed," she said. "Good! Now I want you to push up as hard as you can to lift your body." To my surprise, I rose off the bed and into a somewhat standing position with only a little help. "Great! Let's turn now!" she exclaimed. "Guide with your feet, then let your hips follow." Once I was lined up with the chair, I plopped down in exhaustion.

"We've got to get you using that 85% oxygen saturation as efficiently as possible," the PT said when she returned that evening. "Follow my lead," she said. "Big breath in." We breathe in. "Good! Now purse your lips," she tightens her lips and only partially opens them to show, "And breathe out through your mouth." I take a couple of these breaths on my own as she tells me, "This technique does not allow you to release as much carbon dioxide, to trick your body into taking more deep breaths. Not only will this help keep oxygen levels more stable as you walk, but it will also help you bring them up faster when they do drop." To practice, we went out for my first stroll; five arduous steps to the door of the shoebox-sized room, two steps out, and back. Once, back in bed while being reattached to numerous CVICU machines, I stared straight ahead, thinking I hated walking before, but I could easily make it 100 yards with minimal effort. Now I can barely hobble a couple of feet without feeling worn out. "You just had major heart surgery," my PT, nurse, and parents echoed. "It will get easier."

They were right. The next morning I walked a half lap around the ICU; that night I made a whole lap. The next few days, I was able to make three laps around in a single go. I later moved down to the less intensive "floor," becoming less Star-Trek-Borg-looking with each pacer wire, central line, and IV removed.

June 21st, my 15th birthday. "One . . . two . . . three . . . " I was counting my breaths slowly to keep my oxygen saturation from plummeting this lap. As I turned the corner, with an IV pole in tow, "Happy Birthday to you . . . " erupted from family and friends, along with doctors, nurses, and therapists that had become family.

Realizing the only way to recovery was to walk there, I went on a walk every time I was upset, bored, or excited. It tamed emotions well.

I eased into the physical demands of athletic training while falling in love with the way the body can move, handle stresses, and heal itself. In my junior year of high school, I decided I wanted to be a physical therapist; I wanted to help congenital heart patients regain their strength, lung power, and confidence, like my PT had done a few summers before, for me.

To the disbelief of that blue third grader at recess, I chose to study applied exercise physiology at Texas A&M University.

It was my sophomore year in college, and my single ventricle heart was not handling the three-plus miles of walking I was doing each day. While trying to amend this problem, I was also planning a potential third open-heart surgery that had only a small likelihood of improving my quality of life. To top it off, I had also taken a certain infamous, required class that spring. The class graded on one's ability to accomplish difficult physical activities. I was exempt from the cardiovascular tests, but I developed a gym routine four to five days a week. I worked on strengthening my core, legs, and arms to accomplish modified leg press, bench press, and sit up tests. I left that class in the best shape I had ever been in; I felt strong and confident. My body and soul were ready to take on open-heart number three.

That summer, my surgeons went in planning for a Fontan with a mechanical valve, or a bi-ventricle repair with two mechanical valves. Once in there, they concluded each plan would cause more problems than they would solve. To finish the multi-hour ordeal, they opened my 19-year-old pulmonary artery band a few millimeters, to allow more pulmonary blood flow.

Just like before, 24 hours out of surgery, a PT came knocking on my CVICU door, but this time I was ready. "Do you know how to fire off your quads?" he asked.

"Yes!" I exclaimed.

Excitedly, yet a little surprised, he questioned, "Are you sure? Do you want waist support?"

"No, I got this," I responded. "I did hundreds of squats this spring training for this moment."

"Okay," he said, "On three—one, two, three." With feet shoulder- width apart and a straight back, or as straight as all the wires and tubes would allow, I pushed out of the bed. Less than five seconds later, I was standing, facing the PT, asking, "Can I take a couple of steps before sitting?"

"I really hate to say this," my cardiologist started the following March, "But your saturations have steadied out again at 82%, and the regurgitation through your common atrioventricular valve is still significant and will most likely only get worse with time." I had already figured this out since none of my pre-op symptoms had resolved.

Before the appointment, I had gotten a really great inpatient part-time shadowing position. Though I felt at home in the hospital setting, I didn't have the physical stamina to do the job well for three hours a week, much less every day for eight hours. Though painful, I started looking into other viable careers to help me try to establish pediatric cardiac rehabilitation programs.

"I don't think physical therapy is a realistic path for you," my doctor said.

"I was coming to that realization and was afraid you'd make it concrete," I replied. That ended the idea of physical therapy, and I was mad. Like that blue third grader all those years ago, I was so mad at exercise that I decided I would try to steer clear of it. This time, the boycott only lasted three months. After much research and paper writing for classes, I have realized there is a giant hole in scientific literature on how malformed hearts respond to exercise. Maybe helping to fill in these gaps is the first step. Just because one dream gets cut off, doesn't mean your ultimate end goal is squashed.

Lorrie is a 26-year-old from the Houston and Dallas areas of Texas. She was born with right-dominant complete atrioventricular canal and double outlet right ventricle. Doctors at Texas Children's performed a PA band, Glenn, and AV valve repair to help improve her quality of life.

Since writing her essay for this book in 2018, Lorrie was listed for a heart transplant, graduated from Texas A&M University with honors, completed a Master of Public Health degree in Epidemiology, and received her new, two-ventricle heart after 400 days of waiting.

Lorrie is now attending Physician Assistant school. She can now live all the physical activity dreams she dreamt of while writing her essay, specifically hiking, climbing stairs, and running. When Lorrie is not working as a professional student, you can find her spending time with friends, at the gym, running the Houston bayous, or streaming a comfort show.

Feeling Normal Through Sports

by Michael Hills

I was born in February 1998 in Etobicoke, Ontario, Canada. I have an amazing sister and two loving parents. In August 1998, I wasn't feeling well and was taken to the doctor. The doctor said, "Take him to Sick Kids in Toronto, right away!" They then diagnosed me with a congenital heart defect called hypoplastic left heart syndrome. I had my first of three surgeries shortly after being diagnosed. My first surgery was the Norwood surgery. My second surgery was the Glenn surgery. The third and final surgery was the Fontan surgery. All the surgeries were risky, but I had some of the best surgeons in the world operating on me. I spent months in the hospital. I don't remember any of my time in the hospital and I'm thankful for that. My parents do; I can only imagine what they were going through.

My earliest memories are going to my babysitter Maria's house to spend the day there before I was old enough to be in school. I went for walks with Maria and the other kids all the time. When we got snow and had a winter wonderland, I would play in the snow with the other kids. We made snow angels, snowmen, and had snowball fights.

After my surgeries, the doctors said to my parents, "He won't be able to play hockey or any contact sports, but he will have chances to play other sports." Growing up in Canada and not being able to play hockey was disappointing. Most of my friends and cousins played and loved it. From watching their games, I started to love hockey. The Toronto Maple Leafs are my favorite team. Despite not being able to play hockey, I found joy, happiness, and a sense of normalcy in other sports.

"When I was younger in elementary school getting changed for gym class, other kids would often ask me, "What's all those marks on your chest?" or "How come you have all those marks on your chest?"

I told them, "I've got a heart condition, and all these scars are from the surgeries that were done." After explaining about the scars, they understood and they would sometimes ask about my condition. This happened again in high school. I would get the same questions, and they would get the same answers. Having this CHD has its disadvantages, but I'm proud of the person I am even if I'm a bit different from other people.

I started skating at five and figure skated until I was 18. It wasn't hockey, but I was able to skate on the ice in some capacity. I became a strong skater. Skating gave me exercise to keep my heart strong and healthy. I always came off the ice exhausted, but in a good way, as my coaches gave me a good workout on the ice, especially when I would come from curling all day to my skating lessons in the evenings.

Michael Hills and his coach, Sonya.

Another sport I fell in love with at a young age was baseball. I joined a local baseball league with some friends when I was seven years old and played for 10 summers. Some of my best memories came on the baseball diamond as a kid. I remember one play like it was yesterday. I stole home to tie the game at 5-5! What an experience that was! The game ended in a tie, but it was the closest any team had come to winning against the champions as they went undefeated that season. Playing baseball for 10 summers allowed me to be normal. I was able to run around the bases, get dirty from sliding to make plays, and I took part in activities off the field such as go-karting and playing arcade games.

When I got older, I would join my team at McDonalds after winning a game. Fast-food wasn't the best for me with my condition, and still isn't today, but I'm able to treat myself once in a while. I met amazing people whom I became friends with, some of whom I still keep in touch with today. My friends and I stopped playing after our season in 2017. Despite not being in a league anymore, we get together occasionally in the summer and play for fun, or we go to the Toronto Blue Jays games as we are all huge fans.

When I started high school, I was nervous. I was nervous about gym class in grade nine because I didn't know how the other students would react and treat me when they found out about my heart condition. As it turned out, I had nothing to worry about. The other students were great, and my teacher was amazing. They treated me like a normal student. I took gym class throughout high school to stay active and healthy.

Later, in grade nine, I heard about the curling team at school. I had always watched curling and wanted to try it. Curling is a sport that requires a lot of strength, especially when sweeping the rock. I didn't know how I would do with it, but tried it anyway. I loved it. I loved moving on the ice, releasing the rock, and seeing how the rock curls on the ice. By the time I was in grade eleven, I was on the competitive team taking part in multiple tournaments during the school year.

Throughout the school year, I was playing in curling tournaments for school multiple times during the year. I helped my school team make it to OFSAA twice. OFSAA is the Ontario Federation of School Athletic Associations. It's a provincial championship in Canada. After the 2014-2015 season where we went to OFSAA, they awarded me the Most Improved Player award in boys curling at my school's athletic banquet. My coaches and teammates all said, "Way to go Mike! Great season, well deserved." I will always remember the curling teams I was a part of during high school. They were a lot of fun. I'm glad I tried curling in grade nine.

Outside of high school, I curled at a club. In my last year at the club, my team won the club's Junior Curling Championship. One player on the opposing team was my good friend Josh. It was a close game that came down to the last shot. Luckily, I had the last shot to go for the win. It was the most difficult shot I had ever had to make during my time curling competitively. I got into the hack, visualized making the shot, and took a deep breath before I released the rock. As soon as the rock got through the guards and was going to hit the rock it needed to hit to win the game, I threw my arms in the air, looked over at my good friend Josh and smiled. He knew my team had won. He said, "Congrats Hillsy, that was a heck of a shot and game." My teammates were all amazed that I had just made that shot. They were all saying, "Way to go Mike, what a shot!" It was awesome to win against Josh. We still talk about that game today, even though it has been several years since it happened.

Through sports, I could feel and act like a normal kid. Like most kids, my baseball pants got dirty almost every game (thanks Mom for washing them every time). Most of all, I had fun and made lifelong friends in every sport I played.

Thanks to the team at Sick Kids' Hospital, I've been able to go to college and graduate with a degree in Sport Management; work at a curling club during the winter; work for Jays Care Foundation in the summer, (they are the charitable arm of my favourite baseball team, the Toronto Blue Jays). In the future, I plan to attend another college for a degree in Sport and Event Marketing. I've been able to have a healthy childhood and early adult life. I wouldn't have had these significant memories and opportunities in sports and outside of sports if it wasn't for The Hospital for Sick Children.

Michael was born in February 1998, in Etobicoke, Ontario, Canada. He has hypoplastic left heart syndrome (HLHS). He has had three open-heart surgeries, the Norwood, Glenn, and the Fontan. The left side of his heart was underdeveloped when he was born. He is now living a healthy adult life, a huge sports fan. Hockey and baseball are his favourite sports. His favourite teams are the Toronto Maple Leafs and the Toronto Blue Jays.

Journal Entries

by Alicia Lynch

Tachycardia—June 21, 2010

"Is it okay if I lie down?"

The flutter in my chest started about five minutes ago. I ignored it, thinking it would go away in a few minutes. But now I felt lightheaded.

My friend Katie is understanding, despite only telling her about my heart condition once a few months back.

"Sure! You can lie on the couch. Do you want some water?"

It's summer, and I just graduated from high school. I want to stay in touch with my small group of friends, so when Katie invited me to a sleepover and to watch anime together, I knew I had to go.

The fluttering began after watching Sailor Moon and eating dinner with her parents. I had felt flutters like this before and usually they went away quickly. However, this time, the feeling is lingering for longer.

I lay down on their couch for an hour or two, laying in different positions, but nothing is making me feel better. Eventually, I ask if I can call my mom.

"Hey Mum, I'm feeling a weird flutter in my chest and I'm a little lightheaded. Should I come home?"

My mom agrees I should, and as I hang up the phone, I know she is going to take this seriously. She knows my medical history like the back of her hand, and since I was born, she has always been my biggest advocate.

When she arrives to pick me up, I feel both relieved and nervous. Relieved I am now with my mom, but nervous because I know what happens next.

I ask, "Should we go to the E.R.?"

The lightheadedness intensifies, and I sit back as the feeling washes over me.

"Well, how do you feel? Has the flutter gone away?"

I don't respond, and my mom looks over to see me passing out in the passenger seat.

Going forward—June 28, 2010

I had been at BCH (Boston Children's Hospital) for about a week now, being constantly monitored for arrhythmias. My mom slept on a cot in my room with me.

So far, we learned the cause of the arrhythmia was from a closure device put in by catheterization a few weeks ago. While originally checking my valve pressures, they found a narrowing in my Fontan pathway. They used a balloon to open the narrowing, but accidentally poked a hole. As a result, they needed to put in a closure device to plug the hole. So the flutter I felt at Katie's was atrial tachycardia, caused by the device interfering with the rhythm of my heartbeat.

As I lay in my hospital bed and giggle with my mom about the cute male nurse I had yesterday, a doctor strolls into my room with a surgeon's cap on. He heads to the patient next to me in the same room.

My mom sees him and suddenly recognizes him.

"Hey, Dr. Mayer! Alicia, this is your surgeon!"

I take a breath in, widening my eyes in surprise. I've never met my surgeon, as my last surgery happened 14 years ago, and I was four years old. As I try to think of what to say to the man who saved my life, he taps my foot and addresses my mom and me.

"Hi, oh yeah, so I think we'll go forward with surgery."

My breath catches in my throat, and I stare at him. He nods at us and walks past towards my roommate, the patient he intended to see.

I look over at my mom, tears welling in my eyes. Surgery? I'm going to have another open-heart surgery? I barely remembered my two previous ones, but this one I would remember.

Reconstruction—July 21, 2010

I wake up in the dim ICU of BCH. My blurry eyes focus and I notice a soreness in my throat. I try to swallow, but realize I can't because of a breathing tube in my throat. I peer around, looking for a familiar face, but find none. Tears stream down my cheeks. I made it through surgery, but I am alone.

A nurse walks in and notices I am awake. She places a piece of paper and pen on a clipboard and hands it to me.

"Don't try to talk. Here, you can write on this."

My mind is foggy from the sedative, my body heavy, and I'm seeing double. It's difficult to even hold the pen, but I manage to write something.

It reads: "Where are my parents" in jagged letters.

Finally, I see my mom walk into view. She reaches out to hold my hand.

"Hi honey, you awake?"

I nod my head as crying becomes sobbing. The last thing I remembered was asking a nurse for more calming medication for my anxiety before surgery. And then counting down from 100, waiting for the sedative to take hold and bring me to sleep.

Now, as I awaken, I feel a wave of relief. I was terrified going into this, wondering if I would even wake up. But now here I am on the other side, waking up to see my family.

The procedure they performed is called the Fontan Revision, where they repaired my common atrioventricular valve, and replaced my half man-made and half-tissue Fontan with a 100% man-made tube. This would help with my blood circulation, so oxygenated blood would better be able to reach my hands and feet.

Looking back now, I realize how important this procedure was to my life. I began my freshman year of college only weeks later. In my junior and senior years, I joined the dance club.

Fitchburg State University Dance Show—April 22, 2015

When I'm nervous, I shake. Just slightly, not enough for anyone to notice usually, but enough so I can feel my hands jittering. The anxiety is always the worst right before I'm about to go on stage.

This is my fourth semester being in the dance show. I'm used to being in the spotlight, but the shaking still comes before I step out. This semester I took three classes a week, something I never imagined I could ever do. I'm in the best shape I've ever been in, and I feel phenomenal.

Yet this has still been a tough year for me, because this amount of dancing was exhausting for my Fontan heart. The first few weeks of classes I was sore and worn out as I got used to exercising more, and I took frequent water breaks. Yet I knew it would be worth it when I got to dance in three different numbers at the end-of-semester spring show.

Now that moment has come. I am about to perform in the Lyrical 1, Hip Hop 2, and Jazz 2 numbers. Behind the curtains, I stand in a red sequin tank top and spandex dance shorts. I take a few deep breaths, trying to calm my nerves.

The intro to "Toxic" by Britney Spears plays on the speakers and I step onto the stage, smiling.

Alicia Lynch was born July 3, 1992 with a single ventricle and heterotaxy. Her hometown is Pepperell, Massachusetts. Alicia enjoys yoga and during the pandemic, she even led her family in virtual yoga workouts. A fun fact about Alicia is that she collects unicorn knickknacks!

Journey to Egypt

by Megan Tones

I gripped the railing with both hands and hauled my body up the steep stairs inside the great pyramid. A Japanese tour group grew closer behind me as my "pull step" routine became a "drag step" closer to the top. Far from being a real-life Lara Croft, I stopped for a brief moment to ease the burning sensation in my leg muscles at the threshold of the burial chamber. Inside, different languages echoed off the walls as I looked at the stone sarcophagus where Khufu once lay and imagined how silent it must have been.

It took me a long time to get here, and I'm not just talking about the stairs.

I must have answered 100 questions to be disqualified from travel insurance.

"Does the affected person's skin or lips ever become blue?" "No." Hey, they never said anything about purple.

"Is the person growing at a normal rate?" "I'd say so."

"Will surgery be required in the future?" "I hope not."

The travel insurance clerk looked up at me. "Any other conditions?" "Congestive heart failure."

At this, a hush fell over the room. The clerk's face turned a couple of shades lighter. I felt the stares of the other customers behind me. In their minds, I had become a ghost. I thought of the scene in Highlander when the main character walks into the tavern and confronts the townspeople, whispering about his newfound immortality.

How on earth could somebody have heart failure and be talkin' and breathin'? It's unnatural!

I imagined this to be the thought in every travel insurer's mind over the next few days.

"It's not like old people's heart failure . . . "

"The rest of my heart is fine. There's just a big piece of it missing and that's why it doesn't work so well . . . "

"Last time I went to emergency for atrial fibrillation, they didn't even do anything and I reverted on my own . . . "

There was no use trying to reason with these people, but one gave a helpful piece of advice: "You just need to pass the medical questionnaire."

Armed with this new knowledge, I tried entering my medical conditions into the questionnaire every possible way and found what some might call a loophole: stay out of the emergency room for one year and declare congestive heart failure as the less life-threatening-sounding "impaired contractility."

I was confident that I could stay out of hospital for heart failure. I was in stage two or three depending on whom I talked to. Although my stomach waxed and waned more frequently than the moon, I could manage the occasional flood with a bit of extra Lasix.

Arrhythmias were a different beast all together—for the past two years I'd had violent, bed-shaking fits of atrial fibrillation at the beginning and end of winter that lasted for days. The episodes took a turn for the worse in 2012, and I finally had an ablation in July of that year.

I wish I could say that was the end of my episodes. No longer shaking the bed, they are faster with a more regular rhythm, less frequent, and last only hours. Armed with warfarin, I decided I could wait out any episodes I had while I was away.

I had to agree that few places on earth compared to the majesty and history of Egypt.

Megan and her husband on a camel outside the Great Pyramid

"Haven't you always wanted to see the pyramids and the Sphinx?" My husband was already researching places to go now that I was insurable. There was just one more thing we needed—a guide.

We found many companies offering the tour of a lifetime, but for every thousand excellent reviews, there were a few terrible ones lamenting ruined vacations. Unsure, I contacted them one by one, listing my conditions and requirement for a low-sodium diet and access to blood tests.

The replies came back.

We think our tour would be too strenuous for you . . .

I don't think we could meet those requirements . . .

These rejections led us to a small company by the name of Real Egypt. Unlike the other companies, the owner, a man named Samir Abbass, met with us on Skype and listened patiently to all of our requests.

"I treat my guests like family. I will never take you anywhere that I would not take my wife and children," he said.

I was astounded to see visits to pathology clinics for INR tests slotted amongst the trips to temples and museums. He would also take a satellite phone on our desert tour in case of an emergency, warn me about salty foods, and make sure I drank enough water.

Finally, the big day came. We said goodbye to our families (who hugged us like they would never see us again) and I squeezed my feet and legs into DVT stockings. The last time I wore these, I was recovering from a mitral valve repair. This time, I was embarking on a 24-hour flight to Cairo.

The airport in Cairo was very relaxed, given all the strife we had seen in the news. Security ignored us as we took our bags and walked down a mosaic-lined hall to meet our driver. I scanned the signs and saw one that read "Mr Megan Tones."

"Close enough," I said to my husband.

Outside, we met Samir for the first time. We were familiar with his mix of knowledge, humour, and calm, but not his size. I imagined that he would have to duck and turn sideways to go through a door. These traits came in handy many times when the touts became too aggressive, and even on the odd occasion when I needed practical help.

Our first stop was a visit to a local restaurant for the koshari, a traditional fast food. Made with lentils, chickpeas, onion, tomato, rice, pasta and spices, the smell was very enticing after 24 hours of airline food.

"There are riots five minutes away from here," Samir told us, "but look how calm it is here."

I gazed around at the families talking and eating, some women wearing headscarves and others not, and at the cook flipping a fresh batch of koshari on a gigantic hotplate.

Outside of Cairo, there were fewer tourists, and we explored the temples and monuments in relative solitude. On one excursion to a temple dedicated to the crocodile god Sobek, I watched the galabiya-clad guards carrying rifles.

"Say, Samir," I said. "What do you have to do to get shot?"

He looked down at me and smiled. "Start digging and see what happens."

Every day, I took my Lasix at five a.m. so I could have it out of my system before the day's excursion started. The timing of my warfarin dosage was non-negotiable, and I took it on the backs of camels or while gazing at the hieroglyphics engraved in the walls of the Temple of Seti. I napped in the Anubis shrine of Hatshepsut's temple and on the seemingly endless steps leading to Beni Hassan.

Towards the end of our trip, we flew to Sharm El Sheikh to climb Mount Sinai at sunset, or so we planned. Our guide was a soft-spoken Bedouin man by the name of Salim, who waited with some camels hired to ease our ascent. I knew from experience that they lumbered like the AT-AT Walkers from Star Wars, threatening to topple their riders with every step. With a sheer drop on the outer side of the mountain path, there was no way that I was riding.

Within minutes, I discovered the climb was going to be much harder than I thought. Faint and so short of breath I could barely take 10 steps without rest, I was mildly concerned when my nose began to bleed. My INR must be high. Or maybe it's the thin air. Salim coaxed me with chocolate biscuits and dates as we passed several teahouses, all closed hours earlier. By the time the sun set, we still had a 750-step climb to the summit. I asked Salim if I had been the most difficult tourist he'd escorted up the mountain.

"No. I once had a couple who made me carry their toddler up these stairs. Another man asked if I could hire a helicopter for him."

At nine p.m., we reached the top. Salim took us into a hut where we ate fried potatoes with Bedouins and a couple of European backpackers. The air was so thin I had to try all the heart failure tricks to get to sleep, sitting hunched over, laying on my right side, and raising my upper body. Even my husband admitted he had trouble breathing up there. It seemed that I had only just fallen asleep when one of the Bedouins shouted, "Guests, please get up!" I could not have slept in if I had wanted to—a group of Japanese tourists had gathered in the dining room to read the Bible out loud and sing religious songs. Was it dawn already?

Away from the shrillness of their singing, we took in the sunrise from the top of Mount Sinai. Of course, it was spectacular, but I was still tired and breathless, and my medicine was at the base of the mountain. We descended the Steps of Repentance away from the vendors selling trinkets to ecstatic tourists. On the way, Salim stopped to feed and talk with tired or injured tourists.

"That climb up Mt Sinai was pretty dangerous. Do people have accidents very often?" I asked Salim.

"Oh yes. They have accidents. And sometimes they die."

"Really! What happens? Do they fall?"

"Oh, no, they have heart attacks."

I was glad I didn't know that before I started.

Although it is impossible for me to pick a best memory, or a favourite place in Egypt, two places come to mind before all the others.

The first was Badr's museum in the Farafra Oasis. Built by a local man from desert materials, the museum showcases the artist's love and concern for his homeland. I felt awed and humbled walking inside Badr's creation and was fortunate to meet the man himself.

The other was Siwa Oasis, four hours out of Cairo. A peaceful place with a culture and language of its own. Many of the buildings were made entirely of sand. We were the only visitors at the eco lodge, and we bathed in the hot springs as the staff served some of the most delicious meals we had ever eaten.

It was the trip of a lifetime. And I didn't need the trip insurance even once!

Megan Tones was born in Brisbane, Australia, in 1983. She first caught the travel bug at age six when she travelled to the UK with her family for a vacation. Since then, she has visited a few countries for her research work including China, the USA, Fiji and Vanuatu, and travelled to Japan with her husband. Their trip to Egypt has been their biggest life adventure to date.

CHAPTER 4

CHDS AROUND THE GLOBE

Congenital heart defects are the number one birth defect around the globe. As an American, this is meaningful, but it wasn't until I was communicating with people all over the world that I realized the significance of having healthcare just a car's ride away. When I was putting together the book, *The Heart of a Mother*, there was an essay by Helen Ng, which I absolutely loved. While almost all the women who wrote for that book were not professional writers, Helen was. She was from Singapore.

Her essay was noteworthy because it talked about her family's need to travel from Singapore to the United States for care for her son Paesan. But when Megan and I started dividing the essays into chapters for this book, we discovered something amazing. We actually had stories about people who immigrated to other countries, and they shared what that meant for the healthcare they received in their new homes.

When Lisa Colvil came on my podcast, *Heart to Heart with Anna*, I told her at the end of our recording that I would love to do a program in Vietnamese. We have done several podcasts in foreign languages. She told me she didn't know another person from Vietnam with a CHD. I knew there had to be others, but in thinking about it, I didn't recall any Facebook friends from Vietnam either. Thus began our search. The result: we found Amy M. Le, thanks to the *Vietnamese Boat People* podcast. I did not know how discovering that podcast and "meeting" Amy M. Le would change my life forever. After reaching out to Amy, I discovered a woman with an amazing story and a genuine friend. Since meeting her, she and Jenny Muscatell helped found The Heart Community Collection with me and we've worked with Jenny on *The CHD Magazine*. Her essay, 'Find Your Fierce' will help you understand why she is a force to be reckoned with!

I completely misread Ellen Banoub when I first met her online. I thought she was a quiet introvert. Since she became a volunteer with Hearts Unite the Globe, I've discovered that she actually is a bubbly extrovert! In her essay, we learn about her passion for theater and how, by acting in one play, she hoped for a miracle. Ellen shares with us how God doesn't always answer our prayers the way we thought they would be!

Belén Altuve Blanton has used her heart defect as a vehicle for good. We are like two peas in a pod. Although I am not a heart warrior, I can identify with the quality of Belén's heart. Originally from Venezuela, she is an example of how no matter how far we move from our homeland, there is a bit of our homeland always present in our hearts. Belén has taken her love for the people of her country and worked some miracles. Moving to the United States has probably allowed her to do more good for the people of Venezuela than if she had remained home. I'm so glad she moved to the USA and even happier that she is my friend. Her essay shows how she is a friend to the CHD Venezuelan community, too.

Find Your Fierce

by Amy M. Le

In the summer of 1974, a woman gave birth to the bluest baby underneath the brightest stars and palest moon. Outside the four walls of her hospital room, a war raged on in the humid jungles of the Mekong Delta and concrete jungles of Vietnam. The woman, named Snow, carried her baby for nearly nine months and at 11:53 p.m. she gave birth to a baby girl who screamed at the jarring bright lights, shivered in the cool air, and shuddered at the touch of rough hands as she was passed from one medical staff member to another. No one knew that in the next nine months, Saigon would fall, the American War would end, and communism would reign.

April 1975 came to be known as Black April, but for my mother, Snow, April 30th was a black day for a few reasons. Yes, the Viet Cong won and the American troops pulled out, leaving the civilians fearful of what would happen next, but it was a black day for my young mother to find herself betrayed by her husband as he left Vietnam with his American wife and son. Abandoned, jobless, and far from family, my sweet, beautiful mother quickly learned how to keep us both alive under the new regime.

As a child, I looked alien, with my mottled skin dripping from my small, skeletal frame. I was weak from malnutrition and what little food I ate in war-torn Vietnam was siphoned by the worms in my body because of poor sanitation and spoiled foods. My heart murmur and the hole in my heart compounded all this. It would be another five years before my mother learned that my congenital heart defect had a name—atrial septal defect.

I fell a lot as a child, but not because I was clumsy. I cried a lot too, but not because I was colicky. My body was too frail to keep up with my spirited personality and curious mind. This frustrated me. From the time I was born until I was three, Mama and family members constantly held me. It's a wonder I learned to walk at all or learned the meaning of independence. Cousins watched me like foxes on a chicken prowl to make sure I didn't escape, otherwise a whipping was in their immediate future. Aunties squawked over what I ate or did before I could put anything in my mouth or dash for the door. The only thing more suffocating than the thick tropical air was my family's fussing to keep me alive.

My only reprieve was when I was in the care of my male relatives and their friends. I got a sip of their beer if I wanted to taste it. If I wanted to wrestle with our chickens, it was free entertainment for them. If I wanted to climb a tree, they'd say, "Please get the fruits up there for dear Uncle, won't you?" It wasn't safe outside with the Vietnamese soldiers flexing their military muscles, which looked a lot like AK-47 rifles, but that didn't matter. I wanted to run, to play, and to be normal!

When I was five, after several attempts to escape Vietnam for fear of persecution and starvation, my mother managed to sneak us out of Vietnam along with her 17-year-old nephew and 40 other boat refugees. She had one mission, and that was to safely get us to freedom so that I could have a life-saving operation to fix my heart and patch the hole that was my Achilles' heel. Time was ticking, as the doctors predicted I would not live to see my fifth birthday.

In 1979, after four years of living in fear, risking imprisonment to sell goods in the black market, and fighting to find food day by day, my mama upped the ante. We clandestinely ran from our repressive government in the dark cover of night and boarded a small shrimping boat with other refugees. My cousin, Tri, was in charge of making sure I didn't die. He was always watching over me, touching me, and carrying me. Fear was in his eyes; adventure was in mine. Adrift for five days in the South China Sea, I saw the most alluring sunsets where the sky and water rendezvoused on the distant horizon. My eyes beheld the sharks, dolphins, snakes, and other sea creatures that swam beneath the glistening waters. The birds sang me lullabies while the rain quenched my thirst.

My adventure quickly turned into a crisis. My shipmates moaned and groaned. They complained about the lack of food and the absence of land. Their stomachs growled and their lips cracked. The stench of fear, vomit, urine, and defecation flipped my dreamy world upside down. Then we spotted land.

The small island of Galang in Indonesia became a desolate haven for hundreds of thousands of boat people who were homeless. We were no longer citizens of any country, separated from our family, disconnected from everything we ever knew, and weary of living. We were refugees. The camp was our shelter, but with it came malaria, boredom, crimes against humanity, and hopelessness. In the center of all that was me, a ticking time bomb, ready to explode any minute. Then good news arrived. We were getting sponsored to America!

Amy with her mother, Snow

Shortly after my sixth birthday, five months after arriving in America, they rushed me to Seattle Children's Hospital and I had open-heart surgery. I collapsed as a laggard and awoke as a hustler, energized to start school, learn English, make friends, play sports, and be an all-American kid! I always came in last running the mile at school, but my heart did not stop me from finishing the run, making the volleyball and badminton teams, playing football, foursquare, and dodgeball, climbing ropes, or jumping off a diving board.

Our voyage across the ocean was tantamount to the surgery Dr. Dale Hall performed in 1980. He was a triple-board certified doctor who specialized in valve repairs. Finding him was winning the lottery. Without great risks, there are no miracle rewards. While my six-inch scar initially held me back from feeling confident in my skin, it didn't prevent me from blossoming into the heart warrior I am today.

These days I am an advocate in the Vietnamese and congenital heart defect communities. Thanks to my mother's courage, I found my fierce.

Amy M. Le is a Vietnam War survivor and CHD warrior. She grew up in Seattle and had a successful career at Microsoft and T-Mobile before pivoting to novelist. Amy is the award-winning author of the Snow trilogy: Snow in Vietnam, Snow in Seattle, and Snow's Kitchen. She is currently working on her phoenix series—three books showcasing the resilience of people who've survived deep trauma. Amy is the founder of Quill Hawk Publishing, a woman-owned, Asian-American company that helps indie writers publish their books while amplifying diverse voices through storytelling. She co-founded The Heart Community Collection, a resource for the CHD community, and sits on the board of The Vietnamese Boat People *podcast. Amy also serves as an officer for two writing organizations in Oklahoma.*

Healing

by Ellen Banoub

"Ellen, I found a perfect role for you to do in the play we are preparing for the crucifixion for Holy Week," Michael told me. "It's called *A Space for Crucifixion*."

"Don't you think I will be bad at this since I only do comedy? I am sure I cannot handle a play about the crucifixion," I said.

"Believe me; you will love this role! Something inside me tells me this role is just for you, Ellen," Michael said.

"So, what is this role about?" I asked. I thought the role might be the devil or someone evil.

"The woman who had had a discharge of blood for twelve years," Michael said.

I gasped. All my life, I have been waiting for a miracle to cure my sickness. I longed to be a healthy person instead of a person with a complicated heart—hypoplastic left ventricle with transposition of the great arteries, pulmonary artery atresia, and dextrocardia.

"I have a great feeling, as I am sure the Lord will finally heal me," I said. "I thank you for choosing me for this role."

At the beginning of 2020, my church's acting team was preparing a musical for Holy Week. The play centered on some people that Lord Jesus met, some miracles He did, and His crucifixion. I prayed reverently and read the story multiple times. I meditated on the woman who struggled with bleeding for twelve years. During rehearsal, I got more in touch with the story, sure God would heal my broken heart in the same manner He cured the bleeding woman in the Bible. I did not know anyone with a cardiac problem; I thought I was the only one who had this condition.

I waited for the day of the play to be presented because I was sure that God would do His miracle with me during my scene in the play while I, like the bleeding woman, touched the hem of the Lord Jesus Christ's dress. COVID arrived, and the lockdown happened, so the theatre team could not perform the play. That was a massive disappointment for me as I felt God accepted this virus to come, and the lockdown happened, so I did not get my miracle. I was wrong. Because of COVID, I found different meanings and tests of healing. For this reason, I thought the only solution was to be healed by a miracle; that was my focus.

During COVID, I was terrified of getting the virus, since I did not know how my cardiac issue would react to it. For this reason, I was under significant stress, but my sibling searched online and found Facebook groups for people living with congenital heart defects. Then I joined these groups and listened to Anna's broadcast of *Heart to Heart with Anna.* I contacted Anna and started volunteering with her. I found different healing meanings as I learned more about my condition.

Also, I know many people just like me facing the same struggle. Now I am grateful to God for showing me different kinds of healing. God guided me to see and know that I am not alone; we are many, and we need to help each other in this life. I believe I finally found the purpose of my life that God created me for: to work and help people like me. My favourite sentence is, "You are not alone." Sometimes heart warriors feel lonely in this pain, but that is not true. There is a reason I have this heart condition, which is to help people struggling with physical illnesses. That is how I live beyond my CHD.

Ellen Banoub is an Egyptian who was born on November 6, 1991 with hypoplastic left ventricle with transposition of the great arteries, pulmonary artery atresia, and dextrocardia. Ellen moved to Montreal, Canada nine years ago. She is studying social services and plans to be a social worker. Her cardiac situation helped her choose this career in order to support others struggling with their lives. Ellen has two nieces, one in Canada and one in Egypt. Ellen is the youngest child in her family. She has three heart-healthy siblings.

Little Star of Bethlehem

by Belén *Blanton*

Many years ago, when I was turning 15 (my quinceañera), I had my first heart attack. This devastated my parents, who didn't know if I was going to make it, just like after my first surgery. The dress, the guests, the party . . . everything was ready, but I was fighting for my life. I was in the hospital for over three weeks. It was very traumatic for a 14-year-old who only wanted to live and have her big party.

Well, I made it!

I remember the day of my party, the face of my parents, my family, my friends, and my "other" dad, my cardiologist. I danced the entire night, and everybody was so amazed to see that the girl who was in ICU fighting for her life was having the time of her life. My cardiologist, Dr. Ivan Machado Atias, who saved my life, whispered in my ear, "You are my little star of Bethlehem. God bless you always."

I was born in Venezuela with a heart disease: tricuspid atresia. Every doctor told my parents to let me die in peace, but they never gave up. We had a neighbor who told them about the new cardiologist in town that came back from Texas Children's Hospital and was very knowledgeable about congenital heart disease. They took me there and sent me to Houston, where Dr. Denton Cooley performed my surgery.

Living with CHD is not easy, but it is not impossible. Having the right attitude, faith, and listening to your body are the keys.

Thirty-five years later, I was on disability and unable to work because of my CHD. I said to God, "I know I must have a purpose in life," and my CHD journey started. I joined ACHA, went to the conferences, and started my work as an advocate for my illness.

Two years ago, in the middle of the pandemic, a lady messaged me on my private Instagram page asking me for help. She told me that her baby was born with tricuspid atresia. They were living in Venezuela and did not know what to do. I wrote back with some information about the cardiologists that I knew. After struggling with all the obstacles presented because of their health and living in my country of birth, they lost the battle and died. For me, it was unbelievable! Venezuela has skilled doctors! What's going on?

So I called my "brother," Dr. Machado's son, who is now a cardiologist in Venezuela and a professor of medicine at the most important state university. He told me that 4,000 children are born yearly with CHD, and less than 10% receive the cardiac care necessary.

I thought, 'Thank you, God; I got it! This is my life's purpose!' And just like that, I created the Estrellita de Belén Foundation.

Almost two years have gone by and I enjoy and work like I never have before. These children are my motivation in life. They deserve to have a life like I did.

The most amazing thing is that six months ago a mother contacted me because her 14-year-old was having palpitations and needed to have an ablation because of Wolff-Parkinson-White syndrome. Guess what? She was getting ready to celebrate her 15th birthday, just like me 40 years ago.

That's when I realized, "Yes, this is my mission!!!"

Estrellita de Belén means Little Star of Bethlehem. Those were the words that my cardiology whispered in my ear when he danced with me.

Belén Altuve Blanton was born in Venezuela with a congenital heart defect. Her parents had her transported to Houston, Texas, for live-saving surgery at six months of age. In 2015, Belén became a member of the Adult Congenital Heart Association. Realizing the plight of those with CHD in the USA and Venezuela spawned a desire for Belén to do more for others. She created the Foundation Estrellita de Belén to help underprivileged children in Venezuela. Belén also works with Hearts Unite the Globe as one of the co-hosts of Guerreros Del Corazón, a Spanish-language podcast for the CHD community. Belén has also joined Global ARCH and is part of their communication team.

Endurance

When I was a kid having my surgery in the 1990s there was very little entertainment available. Our choices included playing Alex Kid in Miracle World *on the Sega Master System 2 (someone had stolen the Wonder Boy cartridge from the box),* The Boy Who Could Fly, *or* Conan the Destroyer. *The latter was fairly questionable entertainment for young children, and perhaps that's why we watched it repeatedly (fun fact—Arnold Schwarzenegger had a bicuspid aortic valve so it may not have been completely inappropriate).*

As the youngest in my family with an older brother and older (mostly boy) cousins, I ended up seeing a lot of action movies, and the actors to me seemed to be the embodiment of endurance—taking injuries with an almost robotic calm in the pursuit to whatever end.

While we may not look or feel like action movie heroes (and we certainly don't have their salaries), we endure none-the-less, as do our loved ones who support us. As time passes, the medical field advances and we may find answers to why we feel and experience what we do, or more questions may be raised. My own experience has been that my health has not been linear—I am healthier at age 40 than I was at 26 thanks to medications not available back then.

In the three chapters that form the middle of this book, "Service," "Motherhood," and "Facing My Mortality," you'll meet many others who have endured the challenges that come with reaching adulthood and older age with CHD. In "Service," you'll read about heart warriors working in the medical profession, as well as those who have had valuable experiences giving back to the community or enriching their families' lives.

In "Motherhood," you will learn about the unique circumstances that women with CHD face on the road to motherhood, and how their experiences in growing up with CHD help them to advocate for their loved ones and community. The final chapter, "Facing My Mortality," is a hard read, but so worth it for the wisdom the contributors impart, some of whom have since passed away.

CHAPTER 5

SERVICE

If you've read this book from the beginning, you may have noticed that several of the essays are about helping others. For example, Jason Crutchley volunteered with the American Red Cross to repay all the help he received as a child, while Christy Sillman became a paediatric cardiology nurse within the ICU to help other children with CHD. These stories showed that there were different ways of giving back, and that in giving, you can gain so much.

For example, you may have heard a saying that is some variation of "the best way to help yourself is to help someone else." This chapter expands upon the theme of service.

In Monica's essay, 'Jax: More Than a Service Dog,' the quest for a service dog gives Monica a sense of hope and purpose, Jax a loving home, and both of them loving companionship. Tracey Grasty, Victoria Scoggins, and Roslyn Rivera are all in the healthcare field, reciprocating through their work. In her essay, 'Giving Back,' Tracey describes how she had to stop working as an ICU nurse during the pandemic, and found herself in a different caring role, helping her parents, now aged in their 80s, as they cared for her as a child. In 'My Career Choice,' Victoria talks about the loving guidance of mentors, which steered her towards a career in healthcare administration rather than the frontline. Roslyn's essay, 'Novick Cardiac Alliance Trips to the Middle East and Eastern Europe,' tells the story of her journey from paediatric CHD patient to paediatric CHD nurse—travelling the world to help heal young hearts. My essay, 'Moonlighting as a CHDer' is about a "part-time job" I once had volunteering for a medical school program.

I must admit, I am a bit in awe of my co-authors in this chapter and of what they have achieved. I didn't think I could cut it as a doctor, nurse, or other healthcare professional. However, you don't have to be a medical professional or emergency worker to give back. Even small gestures can make a big difference to somebody's life. Together, these essays show that there are many ways to give back to those in need, and in turn, receive.

Jax: More Than a Service Dog

by Monica A. Mossey

Mid-morning on January 3, 2016, God answered my prayers, but in a much bigger way than I imagined. I was talking on Facebook Messenger when I noticed I had one unread message. At first glance, I caught the words "Therapy Dogs" and "Louis H. Mossey." I stared at the message again and saw a link to check out Therapy Dogs. My heart skipped with excitement at the possibility of my dream finally coming true if Dad was serious about this.

After an intense, internal debate on whether I should inquire, I could no longer stand the suspense; I had to know for sure. Dad was sitting in his recliner when I calmly and nervously asked, "Dad, the message you sent me, does that mean what I think it does?" Looking serious, and not saying a word, he nodded 'Yes.'

I immediately became an emotional wreck; my dream was finally coming true! As soon as I composed myself, I gave Dad a hug.

"Thank you for making my dream come true," I said with a lump in my throat and tears flowing down my cheek.

Still embracing each other, Dad suggested, "Why don't you do some research? There may be some applications to fill out."

"Thanks, Dad! I'm planning on it!!"

Sitting in the living room, I looked at the photo of Levi that was my screensaver. 'Levi,' I thought, 'I love and miss you dearly. You were the best cat anyone could have asked for. I hope you will send me your blessings as I search for a service dog.' I browsed the Therapy Dogs website a bit before I emailed explaining my situation. They responded by telling me their company trained dogs for people who need them as emotional support; therefore, they could not help me and wished me the best of luck in my search. I thanked them and continued researching.

Over the next couple of days, I sent out numerous emails to therapy and service dogs organizations explaining my urgent situation. One-by-one the replies arrived; rejection after rejection. They were the wrong company, required money up-front, or had a two-to-four-year waiting period for a specially trained dog. I could not wait that long; I needed one right away.

"I'm so depressed," I said to my mother. "I don't want to wait two to four years; that's too long. Maybe I should adopt a small dog and train it myself?"

"Keep the faith," Mom said sympathetically. "I am sure God has something special planned. Why don't you email the Milton Veterinary Hospital? Maybe they can point you in the right direction."

I contacted the vet and asked for their assistance. Tears spilled down my cheeks while saying another prayer for a service dog, unaware that my life was about to change the next morning, January 9th.

"Hello. Is this Chico and Friends Saving Dogs? Milton Vet gave me your number. This is Anne Mossey. I'm calling for my daughter, Monica; she is unable to hear on the phone. I am looking for information about getting a service dog for her. She needs a small dog because of her heart defect."

When I woke up, I was shocked to hear Mom say, "Monica, you have to check out Chico and Friends Saving Dogs." Elated and heart pounding, I checked out the Facebook page, browsing through the pictures of dogs available for adoption. I came across a picture of a two-year-old dog named Jax and instantly fell in love with him. "Mom, I am going to inquire about Jax." Mom nodded in agreement. Shaking with excitement, I contacted the owner via Facebook about Jax.

"I told your mother this little guy would be perfect for you!" she replied. Knowing this gave me goosebumps; I knew God was giving me a sign. I scheduled an appointment for the next day since there were three other people interested in him. "Thank you for letting me meet with Jax tomorrow," I wrote on Facebook Messenger. Lying in bed that evening,

I put my hands together and prayed, "Dear God, please help me make the right decision regarding Jax."

The next morning, Mom and I headed over to Chico and Friends to meet Jax. We introduced ourselves and anxiously waited for the employee to bring Jax out. "Here you go," she said, placing Jax in my arms. While holding him, I was unsure if he was the right dog for me. When he laid his head on my shoulder, I had my answer. Filled with mixed happy emotions, I made my decision and adopted a trembling 2-year-old Jax. "Thank you, God," I said, with tears sliding down my cheek.

After Jax settled in and we got to know each other, it was time to begin the training process. I searched online for a certified dog trainer. "Mom," I exclaimed, "I found a trainer!" A couple of weeks later, Maryanne came to my house to meet Jax and me. She asked me what I wanted Jax trained for. "I have a complex heart/lung defect and occasionally wear oxygen," I told Maryanne. "I need Jax to comfort me when I am distressed or sick. Also, I am deaf and wear cochlear implants. I want Jax to alert me when someone rings the doorbell or walks in the house." Maryanne made notes, then pulled out a training workbook, and pointed out the Do's and Don'ts. She showed me how to train Jax to alert me when someone was at my house. "You need to have Jax's leash tied to you for the next month. That's the only way he'll know that you are his owner. It'll also help him learn about your special health needs," Maryanne told me.

Jax was one step closer to becoming a service dog; it was time to get him registered. "Monica," Mom said, "I am so proud of the work you have done training Jax. He seems so much more comfortable with his 'job.' His little blue vest is so cute!" Beaming with pride, I registered him online and anxiously waited for his papers to arrive in the mail. A week later I received them, "Look Mom!" I said upon opening the envelope. "Jax is officially a service dog!" Mom and I cheered. Even though it was legitimate, it did not feel 100% official until Maryanne finalized it.

"I can't believe this is my fourth and final visit," Maryanne said to me. "Jax has been doing great work with his training. I am quite impressed."

"I could not have done this without you. Thank you!" I said to Maryanne as she left.

Jax was exceptional in his training; his intuitiveness amazed me. One day, he followed me around and wouldn't stop crying until I checked my blood sugar. He senses my daily battles and incessant pain by sticking to my side. With his help, although difficult at times, I push through the rough days. He knows what his vest means and takes his job seriously

Monica with Jax

while wearing it. Once it is off, his personality changes from serious to playful; he knows how to keep me laughing. Jax's enthusiasm and zest for life are infectious; he is truly my kindred spirit.

We do not get to choose what happens to us, but we do get to choose how it shapes us. What is life all about for Jax and me? It is about the hope that exists beyond the pain and a journey I never have to make alone.

Monica Mossey was born on September 6, 1984 with Truncus Arteriosus Type II, along with a host of other cardiac and pulmonary conditions. She lives in Vermont with her fur baby, Jax—a Chiweenie dog, who is her pride and joy. She is an avid reader, enjoys doing cross-stitch, and spending time with her friends and family—especially her two nephews and her niece.

Giving Back

by Tracey Grasty

My temperature wouldn't go down. Mom and I were in the emergency room (ER) for the third time. My mom was yelling at the doctors because they thought I had the flu and gave me a shot that didn't work. My fever was up to 104 degrees Fahrenheit.

Mom held my hand and reassured me all would be ok. I remember being so scared because the doctors couldn't help me.

Then Superwoman showed up—a beautiful Black woman pediatric cardiologist. She touched my hand and reassured me and my mother. "I'm going to find out what's going on," she said. She ran tests and discovered I had endocarditis. I was 11 yrs old.

I had to be admitted into the hospital for one month on IV penicillin. As a child, it felt like forever. I knew about hospitals. I was born with tricuspid atresia (TA) with hypoplastic right heart syndrome (HRHS). By the time I was 11 years old, I had had two heart surgeries. One was a Blalock-Taussig-Thomas shunt at 15 months and one was the Waterston shunt at four-and-a-half years old. I remember little about these surgeries except after the Waterston shunt; I remember going back to the hospital to get my stitches out. In a cold room, they took a set of pliers and removed them. "Ouch," I said repeatedly. It seemed as though I had a million stitches.

During my hospital stay, Mom visited every day after teaching school before going home to fix dinner. She sat with me as I ate nasty hospital food and complained about being there. Mom held my hand and comforted me. I anticipated Mom's daily visit, and it always thrilled me. My dad, sister, and brother would sometimes come in the evening.

"Thanks for coming!" I said to everyone. They would leave and my heart would sink every time we said goodbye.

That year, I also started wearing a brace for scoliosis. I remember the pain of how it squeezed my body. I could hardly breathe or eat. It went from my chin to the bottom of my butt. Kids teased me because my butt was flat. They would also trip me in the hallway and laugh, because it was hard for me to look down. My clothes tore from the nails and I was never comfortable, especially in a chair, unless it was upright with no cushion. Every three months, Mom would take me for another brace adjustment because I had grown. When the brace would draw tighter, I would feel like my body was in a vise and it was hard to breathe. I had back surgery at 17 years when they placed a Harrington rod inside my back, straightening my spine. I was free!

In 1999, I taught school and in the summer, I taught at a day care. We all went to an indoor play park and the children, two-to-four-years old, were playing on the slide all by themselves. I thought since I was small, I could get on the slide too, to supervise them more closely. Another co-worker, and a friend who was small like me, also got on the slide. I thought, 'Surely if this 50-year-old lady can get on the slide, so can I!' The slide was a tube and was so fast, I couldn't stop and there was nothing to hold on to.

I wound around fast and furious. I reached the bottom. Ow! One leg got caught on the mat and I flew forward. The other teachers took the kids away so they wouldn't get scared when the ambulance came and took me and my broken tibia and fibula away.

After surgery, my parents came from Detroit to Maryland to take care of me. After a few weeks, Dad went home, but Mom stayed.

We went back to my studio apartment. Mom cooked and cleaned. I had a rod placed so there was no plaster cast, but I had a boot to wear. "Your leg looks like it was in a fight and lost," Mom said. There were bruises everywhere. Physical therapy preserved both legs. Mom stayed until I could take care of myself.

I was in college when I asked my doctor about how long I would live. He replaced my old doctor, who retired. Dr. Ross was straightforward.

"You won't live past 26 years old unless you have a surgery called the 'Fontan,'" he said. I was 22 years old. Mom started crying.

I think that is why my old doctor would hedge and never say how I really was doing. He said, "I expect you'll outlive me!" when he was in his late 60s or early 70s.

I came out of college for the Fontan. All went swimmingly until I felt like I couldn't breathe. I kept calling the nurses and doctors. I had so many tests, but they couldn't find evidence of my decline on any tests. Meanwhile, I asked for more oxygen, which they reluctantly gave me. One night, I woke up and every staff member was around my bed. "Tracey, you look gray. We need to intubate you." I was so scared.

The next thing I knew, I had a tube down my throat. I don't know what hurt more, that tube or my newly operated-on chest. I could hear my mom yelling from the hallway at all the doctors and nurses for not believing me when I said I was feeling worse and having trouble breathing. My mom was hot! That little Black woman telling off every doctor and nurse she could find must have been something to behold.

The Intensive care unit (ICU) allowed 15-minute visits every hour. I looked forward to Mom and Dad visiting me. The ICU was cold, and I stayed in pain. "Morphine," I said to the nurse. All I wanted was sleep. Sometimes Dad couldn't come, but Mom was always there.

A few decades later, I felt my heart beat fast and weird while charting as a pediatric cardiac ICU nurse. I put myself on the heart monitor and couldn't believe my eyes! My heart was beating 250 beats per minute! I was in atrial flutter.

They put me on a beta blocker medication that dropped my heart rate to about 35 bpm. I could barely get out of the bed. I had no energy. I needed an ablation, a procedure where they burn away the areas of the heart that cause the arrhythmias. Before my ablation, I heard a knock on my house door. "Mom! Dad!" They came to take care of me until I had my procedure. A sense of relief washed over me.

Years passed, and I visited home more often because my parents became too old to travel. One day, Mom and I went shopping and as we prepared to leave the mall, Mom couldn't remember which door we came in. I recognized a store and a pillar, so I directed us accordingly. Then Mom couldn't find her car. This never happened. Luckily, I saw a glimpse of a light blue car and went over to it. It was Mom's car! When Mom couldn't find her way home, I knew something was wrong. My phone GPS got us home.

"Tracey," Dad said in one of our regular calls. "Mom isn't paying her bills and her phone got cut off."

"I did too pay them!" Mom said. "I gave them $100 in cash and I don't owe anyone anything!"

Mom's credit score was 850. She was never late with her bills. I realized I needed to help Mom and Dad.

Mom will be 87 later this year and Dad will be 90. I travel from California to Detroit, Michigan at least once a month. When the pandemic happened, I was unable to work my regular job as a pediatric cardiac ICU RN. Since they allowed me to work remotely, I took my computer and stayed in Detroit for several months.

Mom has developed Alzheimer's dementia, and she is progressively worsening. She refuses to believe she has Alzheimer's and will not allow me or anyone to bring a care provider, housekeeper, or anyone in the house. It is part of the disease. When I am home, I do what I can. Dad cleans, cooks, and does laundry. Unfortunately, my sister and brother don't come home to help. They refused to come home during the pandemic, even though I begged them to. I wore full personal protective equipment (a Tyvex suit with a hood, a hairnet, booties, mask, and shield) and traveled in first class on a direct Delta flight because first-class passengers sat alone.

Mom assigned guardianship to me. I started taking care of the bills and paying more attention to her medical issues. Although financially and logistically difficult, I am glad I could do this for her. While I was in Detroit, I got her a mammogram, on blood pressure medication, and a gastroenterologist for her gastroesophageal reflux disease. I helped Dad get his correct medications, appointments, and followed both of their health closely. I still do. Before I left, I made sure they got their COVID vaccinations.

"Here, Mom," I said while helping her dress for her podiatry appointment. "You can't wear a slip and pants. Let's wear this pretty shirt. Let me help you with those buttons. It looks like your arthritis is bad today."

"She keeps hiding her keys and mail," Dad said.

"I do not!" Mom said. "You keep taking my things!"

We both know this is part of the progression of Mom's illness.

"It's time for you to have a nurse and physical therapy," the doctor said at one of Mom's appointments.

"I don't need strangers in my home. I'm fine," said Mom.

I want to help both my parents, especially my mom, not only because they are my parents, but because they always cared for me when I had CHD problems. Prayerfully, I can give Mom and Dad back a morsel of what they have given me.

Tracey Renee Grasty is the youngest of three and was raised in Detroit, Michigan. Tracey was born on September 23, 1966 with tricuspid atresia (a.k.a. hypoplastic right heart syndrome or single ventricle). While Tracey is single without children, she does have a pure white pet rabbit named Snowball. A bird lover, Tracey, also has a Pineapple conure named Sunburst because of her vibrant colors. In the past, Tracey loved to travel and go to live concerts. She followed her favorite living singer, El DeBarge, around the country, attending all of his concerts.

My Career Choice

by Victoria Scoggins

"Victoria, have you thought about your career?" I remember my cardiologist, Dr. Mullins, asking me during a routine follow-up appointment. "Because of your tricuspid atresia and other heart defects, you will have a tough time getting health insurance. It is very important you have insurance that has good coverage, and you can't ever let your policy drop."

At 16, this was not a conversation I was ready for or even wanted to think about. I always knew that insurance was going to be an important aspect when choosing a career. Mom would always say, "You need good insurance," whenever I would talk about the future. From an early age, my parents, pediatrician, and cardiologist always reinforced that I would need good health insurance throughout my life, and a career that fit my physical abilities.

I had an inkling I wanted to work in the medical field—I wanted to be a doctor, but my fear of needles prevented such a vocation. With my frequent visits to my pediatrician Dr. Toland's office, I became a regular there and even had my own room. My pediatrician became a family friend and mentor. Knowing my fear of needles and that I had an interest in a career in health care, he asked, "Have you thought about going into healthcare administration?"

"No, I didn't even know that was an option." He told me to set up a meeting with their office manager and, of course, I did. I ended up working in my pediatrician's office during summer vacation and saw firsthand the duties of an office manager. I decided I was going to be in healthcare administration. Now I sought colleges with a Healthcare Administration program.

Unfortunately, I did not find a college that specifically had Healthcare Administration as a major, so I ended up getting my bachelor's in business administration. During summer vacations, I returned to my small town and because my pediatrician knew the chief executive officer (CEO) of our local hospital; I was able to have a one-on-one meeting with the CEO to further discuss pursuing Healthcare Administration. He offered me summer jobs to get hands-on experience and learn about the administrative process of running a hospital.

While earning my undergraduate degree in business, I signed up for the only healthcare administration class that was offered. The professor of this class retired from a healthcare organization as CEO. He was someone I needed to talk to and get more insight into this career path I had chosen.

"Victoria, if you want to get into Healthcare Administration, you need to think about getting your master's degree," and my professor suggested some universities that had great programs. I took his advice and pursued a master's degree in healthcare administration.

During graduate school, I was in a work-study program with the program director, Dr. Moseley. His background was in hospital administration and his father had been one of the first hospital administrators for the Veterans Administration (VA).

With a year left until graduation, he asked me, "What part of healthcare management do you want to go into?"

"CEO of a children's hospital."

Knowing my medical history, he said, "You should look into Veteran Affairs. They have great benefits and good job security."

Since I had multiple open-heart surgeries as a child, I pictured myself working in a children's hospital. Dr. Moseley offered some good points I would need to consider when picking my first job. Perhaps his greatest contribution to my career decision was recommending that I consider working for the Veterans Administration.

As I got closer to graduation, he asked, "Have you applied for any of the VA Administrative Fellowships? You know there are few offered throughout the country and they are very competitive."

A few days before my final presentation, he asked, "Have you heard from any of the fellowships you applied for?"

"Yes, but I haven't received an offer yet."

He looked disappointed, but said, "There's still time for the facilities to select their Administrative Fellows." The next day, I got the call. I was being offered an administrative fellowship! On the final presentation day, Dr. Moseley peeked his head into my office.

"It's time for your presentation. Are you ready?"

"Yes."

After my final presentation, with most of the professors sitting there, Dr. Moseley asked, "Did you get any offers?"

"Actually, I got an offer yesterday with the VA for a Healthcare Administration Fellowship and I have accepted the offer."

I have been with the VA for over 14 years, and it has been the best career decision. Over the years, I have worked in three VAs in three different cities. I have very good benefits that generously cover my increasing medical care costs.

While healthcare insurance was always the crucial factor in choosing a career path, I have found a career that gives me satisfaction every day. I get to help Veterans and having great health insurance is just a bonus. From Dr. Mullins to Dr. Moseley, and everyone in between, I have had many significant mentors who influenced me and guided me to a successful healthcare career.

Victoria Rose Scoggins was born in 1983 with tricuspid atresia. Her heart defects were not diagnosed until she was one month old, when she was rushed to Texas Children's Hospital for surgery. In 1989 she had the Fontan.

Realizing congenital heart defects needed more publicity, in 2014, she started her Wear Purple for CHD Awareness event on Facebook.

Although originally from a small town in Texas, she now calls Arizona home. She shares her home with her dog and enjoys working her Scentsy business when she's not working her full-time job at the VA Hospital as a hospital administrator.

Moonlighting as a CHDer

by Megan Tones

From the hallway, I hear Dr Smith lecturing the medical students: "When you are taking a patient history for your objective structured clinical exam, you don't have much time, so it's all about pattern recognition . . ."

Out of breath from walking up the hill, I wait in the doorway " . . . You need to look for patterns of symptoms to clue you in on what might be going on with the patient . . . Ah, Megan . . ." Dr Smith smiles. "Take a seat. We were just going to start introductions."

As we go around the room, I learn the students are from different corners of the world. How exciting it must be to move to another country to study and work! On my turn, I try to sound interesting. "My name is Megan. I was born here in Brisbane and work as a rare disease registry curator and researcher. I enjoy traveling and go to Japan nearly every year."

"Megan is here as one of our patient volunteers," said Dr Smith. "She's going to go back a few years to when she was 22 and first presented to her doctor with a new medical issue. Would anybody like to volunteer as Megan's doctor?"

They look at me, already turning over facts in their minds, young, female, working, travelling, and considering possibilities. Finally, a student volunteers and the game begins. My task, to reveal as little as possible about my medical history. I even covered my scar and painted my lips.

"So, what brings you here today?"

I want to say, "Well, a little while back, my paediatric cardiologist told me that my heart has been stable for years and functioning like normal. But I don't believe him because I still take digoxin and my heart randomly races and I sleep all the time and I get puffed out carrying my groceries home . . . But I am also trying to publish from my honours and get my PhD and write a book and . . . Wow . . . It's like I'm trying to live my whole life in a few years."

But I can't. Instead, I tell them, "I'm 22 and I just moved out of home with my husband and dog. I work at a university and will start my PhD soon. When I get home, I just want to sleep. Sometimes I wake up and my face is all puffy, like the moon. And when I carry my groceries home, I have to stop walking up the hill. Sometimes my heart beats really fast for no reason."

Usually, they start down a line of questioning for anemia, pregnancy, or mental illness. Sometimes, they raise their eyebrows at the moon-face thing, but like me, don't realise that it's water retention. Heart failure from congenital heart defects causes fluid to build up in the darndest places.

Most of the time, the student doctor eventually arrives at heart failure. One even asked if I had a history of heart disease, and I played dumb. "Gee, I had a few surgeries as a kid but I'm not really sure what they were, and I still take these little white pills. Guess I should read the box, huh?"

Once class has discussed my possible diagnoses, Dr Smith turns to me. "So Megan, do you want to tell us what really happened?"

I'm back, squinting at the bright lights of the consulting room at the university's general practice. Aside from what I told the student doctors, I also said, "My heart feels really heavy and dull, like somebody replaced it with a brick or wrapped it in a wet towel."

He raised his eyebrows. "I'll send you off for some blood tests. There are a few rare things I'd like to rule out."

"I'm not your typical student patient, am I? I'm more like somebody you might see on that show *House*."

The student doctor nodded. "I don't see people like you every day."

At the hospital, the gastroenterologist studied my liver ultrasound. "Your liver is congested with blood flowing back from the right side of your heart."

Finally! An answer to why I struggled to keep up with the other students and missed my school bus nearly every day, and when I got older, wanted to sleep all the time. I took the results with me to the cardiologist.

Even then, as I sat in his dingy office with my liver results, he performed an echocardiogram and said, "Sometimes, we see liver problems in Fontan patients, but not in patients with ventricular septal defect (VSD). I don't think your heart would be the cause."

I couldn't believe it! I felt like he was treating me like the old maid in a card game! But he did help me, even though I had to take the long way. "We could do a catheter and a stress echo to check your heart pressures and how your heart works when exercising."

As the classical music played, my cardiologist, surrounded by a registrar and a team of scientists, pressed a needle the size of a pen cap into my femoral artery. Thanks to a local anaesthetic, I felt only a curious pressure, the wires bumping into the sides of my arteries like errant guppies, lost on the way to my heart. I thought of strange science fiction and horror films of the '70s and '80s, Tony Scott's *The Hunger* at the forefront of my mind (maybe it was the Hungarian accent of the registrar). I watched my heart on the monitor as the scientists read out numbers. It was almost hypnotic, except when my heart rate spiked a couple of times.

"The procedure's over," my cardiologist said calmly. "We need to remove the wires now."

I looked down as the doctors put a towel over the needle. What happened next was a coordinated effort. As my cardiologist removed the needle, the younger registrar pushed down on the wound with all his strength.

Even so, the blood flowed like a hose on full power. I stopped looking, but felt the towel growing heavier with . . . me. My lower body felt like it was unravelling, my feet detaching, floating away like smoke. I thought of my blood like a magician's silly string squirting from the cuff of a magic jacket . . . how absurd life is. This isn't as much fun as it looks on *True Blood.* When would this end? How?

"Ok." Somebody put a hand on my shoulder and a blanket over my shaking body. "We stopped the bleeding."

It surprised me that I was able to stay on the treadmill for eleven minutes. For the first few minutes, I chatted with the cardiac scientists. "What do you think of *House*?"

"Terrible show! It makes people think that the crazier your doctor is, the better."

My cardiologist called me back a few weeks later. "Your mitral valve is leaking quite a lot when you exercise. We're going to need to repair it."

I had a huge mortgage, four new rescue dogs, and was halfway through my PhD. Now was not the time for surgery. "Can I have it two years from now?"

"I don't think you've got two years."

He was right about that. Soon, I was out of breath chopping a tomato. Or tying my shoes. My dogs became my masters. My husband watched helplessly as I lay next to the window, staring at the world I was no longer part of. Finally, I called an ambulance. In the hospital, a new congenital cardiology team prescribed metoprolol and furosemide. These were, of course, heart failure medications. Only nobody wanted to come out and say I had heart failure. Instead, I was "an adult with heart disease."

On the third day in hospital, I woke to see my surgeon sitting by the window, bathed in the early morning sunlight like an angel. "We can do the surgery in five weeks."

The last time I volunteered, a student asked me a question I had not heard before. "So what happened after the surgery? Do you feel better now?"

"I think I do . . . " I started. "Not better, but more stable. The surgeon was very good and saved my valve, but I still have heart failure and arrhythmias. One time I ran into my cardiologist in the car park and I asked him why he told me not to come back as an adult, and why he didn't warn me about what could happen later in life."

The student doctors leaned in. "What did he say?" asked Dr Smith.

He said, "Years ago, we felt like if we got you through high school, our job was done." and "I thought it would be pessimistic if we told you all those things, and that you might give up on yourself. It's hard to know what to tell patients."

"There you have it," said Dr Smith. "Sometimes, the patient doesn't fit an expected pattern, or the pattern might be still in discovery. Adult congenital cardiology was a very new field at the time of Megan's case."

As the lecture resumes, I leave them knowing they are a little wiser about adult congenital heart disease. Maybe I will see one of them again in a consult room, a hospital hallway, or at my bedside and feel that I am in safe hands.

Megan Tones was born in Brisbane, Australia, in 1983. Her heart condition was discovered at six days of age, but she was not formally diagnosed with a large ventricular septal defect (VSD) until two years of age. She has had four heart surgeries between the ages of four months and 25 years. She has worked on a range of research projects in the areas of disabilities, education and health, and specialises in research methodology. In her spare time, she enjoys helping the CHD community.

Novick Cardiac Alliance Trips to the Middle East and Eastern Europe

by Roslyn Rivera

As the citywide speakers playing the "call to prayer" in Arabic awaken me, I find myself yet again reflecting on how my life has led me to be in Iraq. Having grown up in a suburb of Los Angeles and attending private Catholic school my entire life, I look back and think that I actually grew up sheltered from the real world. This was likely because my parents desired to keep me safe from harm. My parents raised me with fear for my health, like any parent who heard the words "congenital heart defect."

My parents took home their newborn baby girl, who was just diagnosed with congenital heart defects, their own hearts shattered, their minds confused, their hopes in limbo. Despite my unknown future, they raised me as they would any child, but with a tremendous secret—they didn't share my diagnosis with any family! My grandmother cared for me, not knowing that my heart was literally a ticking time bomb, lovingly giving me sugar water when I had a "boo-boo." I still am amazed that my parents kept this secret, wanting family to treat me like a "normal" child. It wasn't until I fell into heart failure at age three that surgeons touched my heart to repair it. From this moment, my heart became the focus.

After my second open-heart surgery at age ten, I knew I wanted to be a pediatric nurse when I grew up. Even with my sometimes-failing heart, there was nothing stopping me. Here I am as a pediatric cardiac nurse working alongside an international medical team to provide free cardiac surgery to children in the developing world. When I graduated nursing school at 21, I did not envision that my future would lead me to a country where the language and culture were extremely foreign.

This humbling life reflection is cut short as the phone rings in my hotel room. "Good morning!" my father said as I answered the phone. Instantly, I am in shock and awe, a state of joy that only my dad's voice could produce. He somehow figured out how to call my hotel in Iraq, from California! Hearing him express how proud he was of me for having the courage and determination to travel to Iraq to provide my nursing expertise, words spoken from halfway across the world, made my heart so full of love.

As my career as a pediatric cardiac nurse advanced, I recognized that congenital heart disease spans the world, regardless of race, culture, religion, politics, or economic status. It became my sole purpose, my passion, to help heal children worldwide, children with CHD, just like me. Not only these children with special hearts but also their parents and families, just as mine were cared for throughout my childhood. My dad was my ultimate supporter, encouraging me when I told him I was leaving California to start travel nursing across the USA; crying tears of joy (and probably fear) when I told him I was now taking my work overseas.

Over the past 10 years, I have taken part in medical mission trips to developing countries such as Iraq, Dominican Republic, Libya, Ukraine, Russia, Iran, and Ecuador. Novick Cardiac Alliance provides free life-saving cardiac surgery to children with CHD and medical education to local teams so that they can become sustainable programs. Having spent a total of over six months in Ukraine and Libya, places I barely remember learning about in school and where I didn't know a single word of the language, I now know these places so well that I could take public transportation, and the medical teams are my friends, who keep a small part of my heart. As much as I may have taught the local teams, I learned so much more about the world, about language, religion, culture, and hope. I have followed my heart's desires, quite literally, across the globe.

As I prepare for my shift in the Iraqi hospital, I tie my hair up and put on a scarf to cover it out of respect. Looking into the mirror, I notice the faint line of my chest scar, and smile. Throughout my travels, the one undeniable thing is that a smile translates in every language.

There are numerous remarkable memories ingrained in my brain: a once blue-lipped child walking out of the hospital, with a beautiful healing scar on their chest and a new hope for life. A grateful parent repeatedly telling me "thank you" in their native language. The nurses I've taught CPR to performing these skills to save a child's life. A mother holding her baby in the ICU, scattered with lines and tubes, noticing my chest scar, and realizing that there was hope for her baby's future.

I believe my heart desired these experiences to feel whole, and I will forever be grateful for being born with CHD.

Roslyn Rivera, BSN, RN, CPN-BC was born 7/10/83 in Los Angeles, California with partial AV canal defect and she had two heart surgeries in childhood.

Roslyn's CHD led her to become a pediatric cardiac nurse. As a nurse, she has worked in 15 US cities and seven developing countries. She enjoys teaching patients and families about their heart condition; especially helping her patients learn to take ownership of their health. Roslyn's father was diagnosed with CHD at age 57, and unfortunately passed away from complications related to his CHD surgery in 2016.

Roslyn volunteers with several CHD organizations: Camp Del Corazon providing year-round opportunities for children and young adults with CHD; ACHA as a Peer Mentor; Conquering CHD as a guest blogger, and Hearts Unite the Globe as a Medical Advisory Board member.

In her free time, Roslyn enjoys camping and hiking with her husband Michael, who is a heart transplant recipient, and their two dogs.

CHAPTER 6

MOTHERHOOD

The Heart of a Mother was an anthology similar to this one that I started working on in the 1990s. When communicating with other Heart Parents, I told the same stories repeatedly—stories of hope and healing. My friend and fellow heart mom, Jane Hunt, told me I needed to put a book together and before I knew it, over 100 women had reached out to me online to share their stories.

One chapter in *The Heart of a Mother* is "Mothers with Congenital Heart Defects." It was one of my favorite chapters to work on. Just the title itself gave me hope. That there were women out there, women like my child, who had achieved motherhood, gave me so much joy. Not all the women could have children naturally. Some women adopted, but that in no way made them less than a mother. If anything, it made them extra-special mothers because they had to go through the adoption process, which is no mean feat!

What I love about the upcoming chapter on motherhood is that it contains essays that tell about so much more than motherhood. In Karla Deal's essay, we learn about her achieving motherhood, not once, but twice! How does a woman with a serious congenital heart defect achieve such a feat and desire to do it a second time? Even some women with healthy hearts sometimes decide that the work entailed to carry and then care for a child is too much. How much more difficult is it for someone with a serious CHD?

Megan Hanshew's mother was one contributor to *The Heart of a Mother.* Shiloh Hanshew wrote for the "Moms in the Military" chapter and she talked about the challenges of raising a daughter with a serious CHD while her husband was in the Air Force. Megan's essay is an homage to her mother and a memoir of her own venture into motherhood. We certainly see Megan's own growth as a woman, and her and her mother changing from a mother-daughter to mother-mother relationship.

What I absolutely love about Gwenyth Murphy's essay is how it's two heart mom stories in one. Not only was Gwenyth born with a CHD, her mother was as well! Gwenyth's essay takes us back and forth through time when CHDs were almost uniformly fatal. How this woman's relationship with her mother blossomed over time! Gwenyth shares the lessons they have learned in this touching essay.

Kimberly Russell knew from an early age that she would adopt her daughter someday. In this essay, she shares an excerpt from her book *In a Heartbeat* and tells us her adoption story.

The chapter concludes with an essay by Tracie Wendorf-Salgado about a life-changing experience she had as a mother. Sometimes mothers need angels in our corners and Tracie was lucky to have one in hers one day when she and her son could very well have lost their lives. If you need some inspiration, you won't want to miss Tracie's essay.

Motherhood and CHD

by Karla Deal

As a woman born with a complex congenital heart defect, one question can easily loom over all others as we grow into womanhood: Can I successfully have a baby? One question might not necessarily enter one's mind, though—"Is it possible that a pregnancy just might save my life?"

I was born with tetralogy of Fallot (ToF) in 1984 and had a total correction for ToF at nine months. After being told this operation "fixed" me, I stopped being seen by a cardiologist when I was six. Just before I was 18, I asked to go back and see the cardiologist. Deep down, I knew something wasn't *right*. Sure enough, during that appointment, I learned there are no fixes or cures for CHD. I always have been, and will always be, a CHD patient. I began being followed by a pediatric cardiologist.

It was a chilly January morning when I learned I was going to be a mom. My pediatric cardiologist had been having "the talk" with me since my reintroduction to care when I was 17. It was the you-should-consider-having-a-baby-while-your-heart-can-still-tolerate-a-pregnancy talk.

I know, not your usual late teen chat, is it?

By 22, I was expecting my first child. Will I be a wonderful mom? Am I financially prepared for this? What are the best parenting books? While I shared those common new-mom concerns, there are unique issues when you are a CHD patient. Will my heart tolerate this pregnancy well? Will my children inherit my CHD? Will I have the energy? My cardiologist reassured me that all would be well and the only recommendation for my pregnancy was to receive an epidural during labor.

So, I chose an OB/GYN at the nearest hospital. Who wants a long drive when she goes into labor? Like many expectant mothers, I had plenty of questions and concerns. Some were common and answered easily. However, the questions I had that concerned my CHD remained unanswered. At one point, my cardiologist even admitted, "Pregnant women scare the hell out of me! There's so much I just don't know!"

To our joy, my husband and I welcomed a healthy son! Then on a January morning two years later, we were expecting again. This time, I knew something was wrong with the care I received during my first pregnancy. That same gut feeling drove me to seek answers. After receiving a referral from my primary care provider, I saw a general cardiologist. This cardiologist took one look at me and said he wouldn't take me on as a patient. He referred me to the Adult Congenital Cardiology Clinic. I never knew there were cardiologists who specialized in treating adults with congenital heart disease!

During my first appointment with my adult congenital heart disease (ACHD) cardiologist, I was introduced to the Adult Congenital Heart Association. My ACHD cardiologist also taught me more about my prognosis in one appointment than I had learned in seven years from my pediatric cardiologist. She referred me to a high-risk OB/GYN who had a lot of experience treating patients with CHD.

My new OB/GYN wanted to know if my medical team took any special precautions during my first pregnancy. I shared with her they had given me extra fluid in my IV to "help my heart flush things out." To my surprise, both my OB/GYN and her nurse in the room were stunned. Their jaws dropped before they gathered their composure to inform me what a terrible mistake my previous OB/GYN had made. That extra fluid could have overworked my heart. My stomach turned when the nurse bluntly said I could have died. They assured me they would do the exact opposite, measuring my output.

With great delight, we welcomed our second heart-healthy son! As it would turn out, I found myself in proper care just in time. Our sons were just four years old and one year old when my ACHD cardiologist said it was time to replace my pulmonary valve. Frankly put, they don't perform open-heart surgery because you're well. The months before my operation were as physically challenging as they were emotional. I went into that surgery knowing it would save my life or take it. I spent the weeks before it preparing for either outcome.

It's difficult to put the evening before my surgery into words. My surgery eve made a greater impression on me than the surgery itself. I made sure I put the boys to bed myself. The best-case scenario was that I wouldn't be able to do this by myself for about eight weeks. The worst case was that it was my last opportunity to hold them. Some may think I was being negative admitting that to myself. Or even unwise. But I don't think I was at all. It was a possibility, and a possibility I was going to prepare for. If this was my time, it was going to be a special time spent with my babies. I held my one-year-old until he fell asleep and cried when I had to put him in his crib. Pulling myself together, I fought the lump in my throat as I read my four-year-old a story and played with his hair while he fell asleep. I wept and prayed over them as I savored every minute I could that night.

Early morning came, and I took one last peek at my sleeping babies before my husband drove me to the hospital. After being prepped, we said, "See you later." Then I was wheeled into the operating room. My wonderful surgeon took my hand and said, "Don't worry, I'm going to get you home later to those boys." In his wisdom, he said the one thing he knew would motivate me the most. In kindness, he brought the most precious people to mind just before he gave the anesthesiologist the nod to put me to sleep.

Recovering from open-heart surgery with two little ones may be the hardest thing I will ever do. I will never get back the seven weeks I couldn't hold my baby. Or the 10 weeks before I could hold my four-year-old. I often wonder if I would have found proper care in time without that second pregnancy. Perhaps. However, motherhood brought me to the proper care that every CHD patient needs. Motherhood saved my life. I'm thankful for that season of my life and for all the people who helped my family during that time. I'm forever thankful for the ACHA, my ACHD cardiologist, medical team, husband, and most of all, my precious boys.

Karla Deal is a tetralogy of Fallot patient living in Yulee, Florida with her husband and their two children. She had her first open-heart surgery for a total correction for tetralogy of Fallot at nine months, followed by another to replace her pulmonary valve at age 28.

At age 38, she had a heart catheter to replace her pulmonary valve. She recently moved with her family from Washington State to Florida. She has embraced her new home by learning how to surf. So far, she's fantastic at falling off the surfboard.

Like Mother Like Daughter

by Megan Hanshew

"My water broke!" I said to my mother.

"What? It's too soon!" she exclaimed.

That was the beginning of a six-week stint in the hospital while we waited to see how long I could keep my son inside of me so he could continue growing and developing as much as possible. It's hard to believe that happened 13 weeks ago. Seven weeks ago, I gave birth to Charles. A few weeks before, I was told I would have to be admitted at some point because I did not have enough amniotic fluid to go to term. At 24 weeks gestation, my water broke, and I went into the hospital.

The first three days, I had IV antibiotics and three iron infusions in three different/separate IVs. I told the nurses I needed a smaller needle with my IV and they finally listened. They did an ultrasound every Friday until I started having contractions. They weren't consistent contractions, but that they held off until four weeks after my water broke was pretty amazing. Fast forward two more weeks and he was born at 31 weeks and three days—two months early.

He was in the neonatal intensive care unit (NICU) like I was as a baby, but his stay was longer—30 days compared to one week. But that was just the beginning of our journey. While in the NICU, Charles was on antibiotics and nutrients through an IV for the first four days and on continuous pulmonary airway pressure (CPAP) for the first five days. He got fortified breast milk for the first three weeks, then got put on 24-calorie formula.

When Charles came home, he was off his feeding tube and was having no issues. After the first few days of being home, I noticed when Charles would eat, he sounded congested. It all went downhill from there. After a week and two days at home, Charles got admitted into the hospital for breathing issues and they put him on four liters of high flow oxygen

(O_2) at room air. By seven a.m. the following day, Charles was on 12 liters and since there was no change in his condition, they sent him to the PICU, where they put him back on CPAP. After being in the PICU for a day and a half, Charles had his feeding tube back in, but after a week, he started having issues with feeding. About a week into the hospital stay, Charles had a swallow study done that showed he had microaspirated and had dysphagia.

Despite all these issues showing up, Charles was improving. He got down to 1/10 liter of regular oxygen and was ready to go home two weeks later. Devastatingly, that night, after spitting up, Charles choked

Megan today with her sons, Charles (front)

and aspirated. His amazing night nurse saw Charles' breathing change drastically and put him back on four liters of high flow at 30% oxygen since he was having trouble breathing room air. Since Charles couldn't handle nasogastric (NG) feeds anymore, his tube got moved to a nasojejunal (NJ) tube. A week later, things were looking up. Charles was on two liters of high flow room air, but his tube curled into his stomach so that had to be fixed and Charles was on antibiotics for aspiration pneumonia. With no end to being in the hospital in sight, life got tough until Charles was off all respiratory support, but then his tube curled again. After they fixed that and put him back on high flow room air for four more days, he was almost ready to come home. His medical team didn't want to send us home with an NJ tube, but did anyway.

They discharged Charles on 8/3/2018. While in the hospital, I constantly advocated for him. I would tell the doctors every day something more was going on, but when they finally listened to me, it was almost too late.

Every morning when Charles was sick, the doctors would come in and turn his oxygen off and his oxygen saturation level would drop into the 80s. I kept telling them it was more than just him being sick and finally the doctors listened to me when he got a fever. They discovered Charles had aspiration pneumonia. I don't think the doctors would have found out if I didn't keep mentioning there was something more wrong every day.

This reminds me of all the stories my mom told me of my time in the hospital as a baby. My mom had to explain that my oxygen was low because of my heart and the doctors wouldn't listen, but once the doctors finally realized it was my heart, I got the care I needed. My mom was my biggest advocate even when I was a teenager and we had moved and she had to explain my surgeries were tweaked specifically for my heart, but my pediatrician wouldn't listen. Being an advocate for myself now can be hard, but I now have to be strong because Charles is depending on me.

Megan Hanshew was born March 19, 1996 in San Antonio, Texas with tricuspid atresia. She was born with no tricuspid valve and no right ventricle. Megan has had three heart surgeries and several procedures in order to live with a single ventricle heart. She grew up in a small town in Texas called D'Hanis with lots of dogs, cats, and she even took care of cattle on her ranch until she moved to Washington state at 13.

Live your Life (with CHD)

by Gwenyth Murphy

When I initially signed up to write an essay about my mother's and my experiences with congenital heart defects, my mom was getting ready to move in with my family and me. A big step for anyone that knew her. Fiercely independent to a fault is a good way to describe both of us. She absolutely loathed feeling as though she was a burden to anyone. Even though she tried many times, she never learned to drive. She just never could get past the anxiety. Instead, she took public transport independently until her mid-60s—and then she had a cardiac event that ended up making walking difficult. Since she was unsteady, I started taking her to her appointments, which she felt bad about. Our cardiologist solved the issue by simply coordinating our appointments and echoes. They were the same day, one right after the other.

When my mom moved in, in August 2018, neither of us expected she would be gone by the beginning of January. To get to that January, we need to start with when she was born.

My mom was the oldest of eight children, born in a small town in Wisconsin in 1949. Back then, the technology simply wasn't there to identify her heart defect. I remember Grandma telling me once that the doctor who delivered my mother said nothing about her heart. It wasn't until a few months later that anyone even mentioned there was something wrong. They could not figure out what it was, and so they did what was the norm for decades to come—they took a wait-and-see approach.

The theory Mother remembered the cardiologists proposing was that maybe she had been a twin, and there was a mirror effect causing the weird heart sounds. Maybe she had tetralogy of Fallot. In any case, she spent summers going on the train to Milwaukee to see the cardiologist there and undergoing catheterizations, which were considered major procedures, not relatively standard as they are now. Finally, around 1975,

Sharon with her brothers

technology had advanced just enough that doctors could finally diagnose what was wrong with her heart. Congenitally-corrected transposition of the great arteries with associated atrial septal defect (ASD), ventricular septal defect (VSD), pulmonary stenosis, and aortic stenosis. "cc-TGA with all the bells and whistles" was how she described it.

In June 1976, my mom had her one and only open-heart surgery (OHS). I don't know if they just did things to last, or if she was just that stubborn to not need another repair. In 1976, heart-lung bypass machines were still relatively new, especially in small-town hospitals, so it was a big deal to have this surgery. Now, for her defect, people can opt for the "double switch" operation. In the end, they patched a dime-sized ASD. They left everything else alone, deciding that they worked for her heart. As was the norm back then, they declared her fixed and sent her out to live her life. Seeing the cardiologist only once a year or so. My mom lived her life, which showed me how to live mine.

I was born 15 months after my mom's OHS. I was born at 31 weeks' gestation. Ultrasounds during pregnancy did not happen too often, and fetal echoes were unheard of. Her doctors had planned on a scheduled Cesarean section, but I had other plans. The doctor had to use forceps because I was in distress and I was small. I was born just three pounds and three ounces, with apparent heart issues.

Two things happened when I was born—things that I heard repeated over and over enough as a kid that they are ingrained. One, the doctors informed my grandparents that while my mom would be okay, to not hold out much hope for me. They really did not expect me to make it through the night. Second, the team had my mom's cardiologist paged out of a keynote address he was giving at a cardiology conference to decide if they needed to helicopter me down to Children's Hospital in Milwaukee. Apparently, once he heard whose baby it was, he said, "Oh, she'll be fine like her mom." That independent, stubborn streak is strong. They ended up not sending me to Milwaukee. I spent two months in the Theda Clark NICU before coming home at just over five pounds.

As with my mom, they opted to take a wait-and-see approach for me. While my mom's defect was more structural, mine is primarily electrical. My primary heart defect is congenital complete heart block, or 3rd degree AV block. In my 30s, my cardiologist determined my aortic valve to be a bicuspid valve. Mine has three leaflets, just one is undersized and fused to another. Now it's the standard of care for babies with my defect to have a pacemaker implanted. However, in 1977, it was not possible to implant a pacemaker into a three-pound baby. After all, they had only developed the first pacemaker with a lithium battery in 1974. It was the size of a pack of cigarettes. So, we waited.

When I say I got lucky, I mean very lucky. My heart had an escape rhythm. The way complete heart block works is this: the upper and lower chambers of the heart can't talk to each other, which can result in a cardiac arrest. The body has a "back-up pathway" in the ventricles, but mine meanders on its own way. I heard it described at a conference once as the atria beating along as it should, and the ventricle follows along like a cymbal player, "Oh, yeah, I should do something."

My back-up ventricular pacemaker chugged along while we waited for devices to get smaller and more stable, and for me to get bigger. I stayed very petite for a long time, probably because of having a heart rate in the low 40s and 30s. It excited me in 8th grade when I broke 80 pounds, and in high school when I finally broke 100.

While we waited, my mom and I just lived. I learned early to listen to my body as far as my limits, just as my mom did. I learned that having a heart condition was secondary to me as a person. When I was eight years old, we moved to Milwaukee, which until that point had always just been a place my mom visited as a kid for heart check-ups.

In the summer, we would walk to the lakefront for a variety of ethnic festivals. Irish Fest, German Fest, African World Festival, all of them. Irish Fest was the one we visited every day when it was open. The walk to the festival grounds was easily two miles, and we probably walked 5-10 miles back and forth on the festival grounds every day. We walked everywhere—across a long bridge to the library, downtown to the museums, and from a bus stop into the baseball stadium. We walked a lot.

From age 12 on, my cardiologist started checking each year to see if this was "the year." I remained stable until my senior year of high school. Although, in hindsight, I do not know how I managed. I definitely did not have a normal high school experience. I was in bed by eight p.m. every night and could easily sleep 16 hours. But that was my normal. As long as I was ok with it, and stable, we put off the inevitable.

It was probably all the walking that kept us both in good cardiac shape for a long time. Along with some luck, we were able to wait until pacemakers had come down a lot in size; and had better lithium batteries. I was 18, and just about to leave for college when I got my first device. College would have been impossible without getting my device, and the longer we waited at this stage, the more likely I was to have a Stokes-Adam attack or other complications. While my stubbornness had gotten me that far, my pacemaker would get me even farther. The biggest change for me initially was that a fog had been lifted. I could stay awake past eight p.m. That was a change. I had no problem walking for miles, but

I never could run far. Now, I could at least attempt it.

At some point, a cardiologist told my mom that she no longer needed to see him. She was not even supposed to be alive, and so whatever she was doing, she should just keep doing it because it was working. So she kept visiting the festivals, hosting enormous feasts for friends, and feeding roommates and friends I brought home for Thanksgiving. I don't think she saw a cardiologist again until I found out about a new specialty for adults with congenital heart defects in my mid-twenties.

She had to be dragged to the first appointment. I had found the sub-specialty by a combination of pure chance and frustration. As an adult, I needed a cardiologist because my cardiologist had passed away. After being told similar things my mom had been told by regular cardiologists I had seen attempting to establish care, I got frustrated and called Children's Hospital of Wisconsin. I was told that they had a brand-new program just for adults with congenital issues. So, I made us both appointments.

My mom was pretty well sold on the idea of never seeing another cardiologist by that point, but she went. When he wanted to do many things, and finally go in and fix the valves and VSD that were never fixed during her original repair, she told him, "Absolutely not." My mom got her way. She would tolerate putting in a pacemaker/implantable cardiac defibrillator (ICD) combo device, but that was it. Somewhere in all those years of not seeing a cardiologist, she had developed complete heart block (common for cc-TGA patients), and A-Fib. She grudgingly started medications, and would tell me they helped, but she didn't want to admit it to our new cardiologist. She didn't want him to be right.

Finding a doctor who understood us and our issues extended my mom's life. With medications, a pacemaker, and follow-up, she kept on doing the things she loved like the festivals, reading and re-reading Tolkien, and making fancy menus for feasts with friends. My mom and I were always close, and I often helped with the food preparation for the fancy menus, and we always went to the festivals together. My mom taught me through showing me that my heart condition was secondary; it is just a part of you but does not define you. Sort of like *Finding Dory*, you just keep swimming. That's what she did and what I did.

Just before Thanksgiving 2018, my mom suddenly got really puffy and full of fluid. While according to her medical records, it was surprising that she was doing as well as she was; she had never gotten puffy and swollen. While she was in the hospital for this, she made a rounding resident chuckle because she told her she had to get home. Why? She had to make the Thanksgiving pies from scratch, of course. I don't think I ever ate boxed food until I was on my own at college. The resident thought she was joking, but she was completely serious. With that stubborn streak, she got enough fluid off to get discharged. She came home, and she showed me how to make the pie crust and the fillings for the pies again.

She ended up going back to the hospital for another brief stay a few days after the holiday, but came home and we filled our days making cookies and bread for my husband and son. Christmas candy for the holiday was our routine. We would get up, get my son off to school and then plan what we would make that day for 'our boys.' On the day that she passed away in January, that is exactly how our day started. I was going to try to get some things done around the house, but I was tired with that kind of exhaustion that only CHDers understand. She planned to make some chocolate chip cookies for 'the boys,' at around two in the afternoon. She chose that time so that they would still be warm when they came home from work and school. That's what she did, and all seemed to be the status quo that we had become used to.

I was starting dinner, and she was on her third batch of baking cookies. We sat down for our break. It was sort of a joke amongst us—"We have done some activity, now let's rest a bit." It was something we had done thousands of times throughout the years. This was part of the knowing-your-limits advice that my mom taught me; I needed to take frequent breaks. So we sat down for our break. My mom mentioned she might want to go to the hospital once everyone got home because something was off. I went to get my phone from the kitchen to check something. By the time I came back, she had collapsed on the sofa. I called the paramedics, but I knew. They worked on her for a long time and then they took her to the nearest hospital, not our usual one. I knew before they left—she was gone, but of course I didn't want to believe it. Until the very last moment, my mom was *living* her life.

I was not expecting this to happen. I knew at age 69.5 my mom was not old, but it was surprising for someone with her bells-and-whistles defects to live as long as she did. She had really been looking forward to turning 70. I think that was her goal, just to make it to 70 and then she would be ready to go. Even though it was sudden, it was best for her. Our cardiologist even commented that her quick passing was the best way for her to go. A long illness in the hospital would not have been what she wanted. In hindsight, I think it was that same stubbornness that got her home from the hospital and kept her from going back until it was time for her to shuffle off this mortal coil, to use one of her phrases.

My mom lived her life doing what she wanted until the very end—backwards and weird heart be damned! I will continue to live my life as she taught me. I think that is really what all patients with congenital heart defects should do. Live their best lives, even if it is sometimes hard to push through each day. Value the small things, like baking a loaf of bread from scratch, or making cookies for loved ones. Take my mother's advice: *Live* your life.

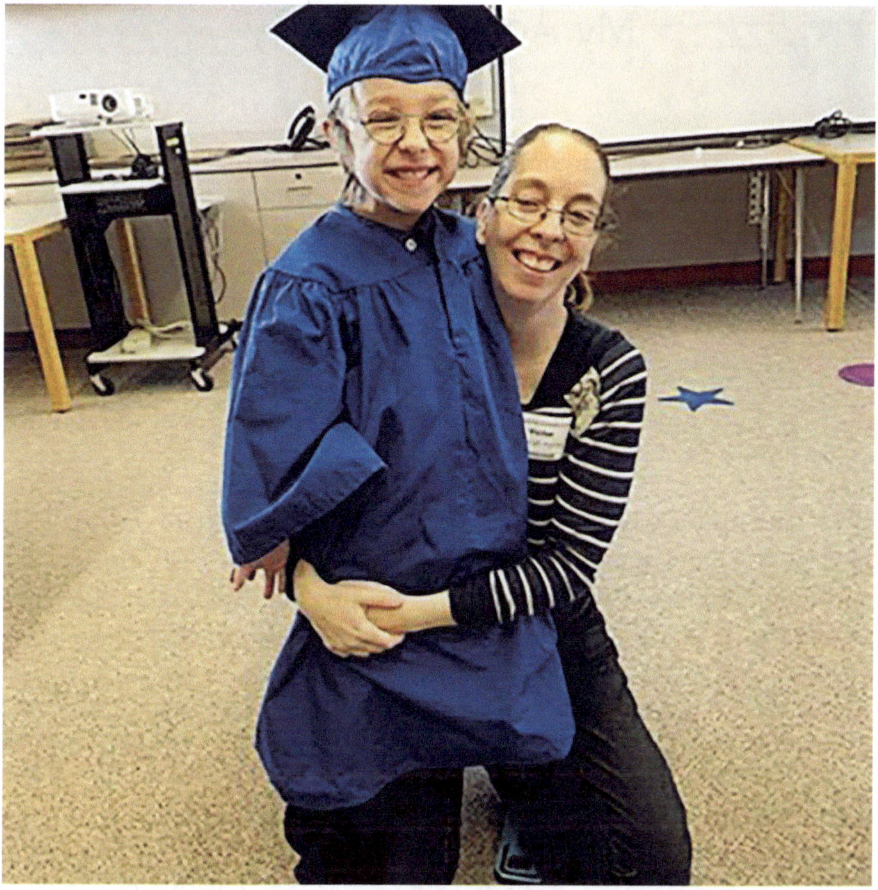

Gwenyth with her son Tyler

Gwenyth Murphy is a second generation CHD survivor, born in 1977 in Neenah, WI. She graduated from Beloit College; and currently lives in Milwaukee, WI with her husband, Joe and son, Tyler. She enjoys photography, various fiber arts, and other creative outlets. She is also working on finishing her mother Sharon's last project, a cookbook of family recipes.

My Adoption Story

by Kimberly Russell

From as far back as I can remember, I have known that I could not give birth. Here is an excerpt from *In a Heartbeat* (the book I wrote about growing up with congenital heart defects):

"Because of the type of heart defect Kim has, there is quite a bit of pressure in her arteries. Cardiologists are recommending that children with this heart defect not bear children. Between the lack of oxygen and the high blood pressure in her heart and lungs, the lives of the mother and baby would be at risk," my cardiologist explained.

Betty (my mother) blinked and stared at the doctor. What was he telling her? Her daughter could not have children? Growing up, getting married and having children were every girl's dream. She frowned and leaned forward in her seat, trying to make the doctor realize what he had just said. "Did you say 'no children'?"

The cardiologist positioned himself so he could look my somewhat-stunned mother in the eye. First, he called her by name. Her head moved toward him. "I did not say Kimberly could not have children. I said she should not give birth to children. Adoption is a very precious means God uses to get the right children to the right families. It is a wonderful fact of life."

His words were so true!

Before my husband and I became engaged, we talked extensively about the seriousness of my heart condition and the fact that there was no guarantee of how long I would live, and that we would adopt instead of having children naturally.

"I know your medical situation. There is no way to predict the future for anyone. God has taken care of you so far. Why not enjoy what we have and wait and see together? And as far as children, adoption is a great idea. Like you said when you were little, 'God has a special little girl picked out for me.' You don't need to worry about any of that. I know all about the baggage. And yes, I love you!"

Just like that, we were engaged and later married.

Ten months later, we got a phone call. "Hello? Mrs. Russell?"

"Yes?" I replied with a curious tone in my voice.

"You don't know me, but someone you know told me you are interested in adopting a child." This brought me right out of bed and onto my feet, while my husband woke up somewhat dazed.

"Are you still interested?"

That was the beginning of our adoption process. The birth mother was only four-and-a-half months along and would give birth in November. This gave us time to prepare. One of those preparations was doing some brief interviews of people that had been adopted. The questions were, "How old were you when you found out you were adopted? How did that make you feel?"

An overwhelming reaction by people who found out in their teen years was resentment and lack of trust. "They lied to me all those years," one lady responded. This helped us in our decision to make the adoption open and natural.

From *In a Heartbeat:*

> The soon-to-be parents were busy finishing the details in the nursery when the phone call came. Their daughter had been born. They could pick her up in two days. Two days later, the young, excited parents arrived at the hospital to pick up their little girl. Kim commented on how surprisingly calm she felt. That all changed the minute the hospital doors opened, and she saw her new baby girl. She broke out into tears as the nurse handed her tiny daughter over to her. The proud father grinned from ear to ear, breaking into his own tears while staring at this new little member of the family. "Thank you, Jesus, for our little girl, Stephanie!"

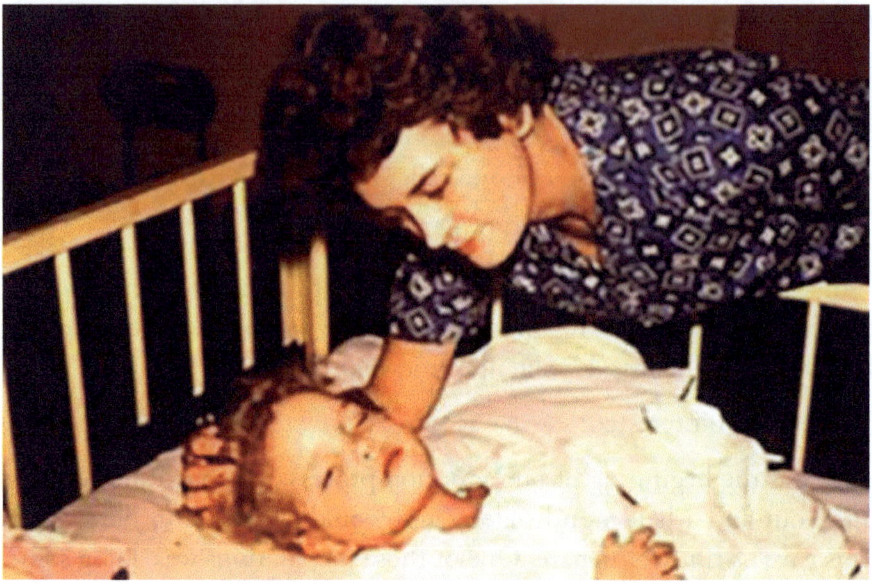

Kimberly and baby Stephanie

The joy of receiving and raising this young child was incredible. She has always been Daddy's little girl and a thrilling joy in her mother's heart. From the time she came home, adoption was an open and natural topic. Stephanie never really asked questions, so when she was seven, we explained what adoption meant. "God wanted you in our family and Mom could not give birth. So He let someone else give birth to you." Stephanie was satisfied with the explanation.

Although it was a natural and open topic, adoption was never really a topic of discussion.

When I tell this story, mothers will sometimes give me a pat on the shoulder and tell me, "I'm sorry you could not give birth."

My typical reply is, "I'm sorry you didn't adopt, because they are two unique experiences, and I would not trade my daughter for the world."

Adoption is an outstanding option for anyone who cannot give birth. When my book first came out, I talked to a girl who found out after she was married that she could not give birth. I gave her a copy of *In a Heartbeat* to let her read about our experience of adoption. A few years later, I called to check on her. "Kim, they are my very own, just as you said."

Now my daughter Stephanie is grown and out on her own. She married an older gentleman with a ready-made family and blessed us with three grandchildren and six great-grandchildren. We love them all!

Kim and Stephanie with their husbands

As a 62-year-old survivor of a double-inlet, single left ventricle (DILV), pulmonary stenosis, and chronic cyanosis, Kimberly Russell has written her story about growing up with a congenital defect in her book, In A Heartbeat. *She and her husband volunteer at Egleston Children's Hospital, both in their in-patient programs and Camp Braveheart. As a former Board member for the Adult Congenital Heart Association, she started a local CHD group in Atlanta to promote CHD education, social events and fundraising for the scholarship program. She and her husband live in Atlanta and enjoy traveling, reading, and spending time with their grandchildren and great-grandchildren.*

Mommy. Mommy, I Thought You Died!

by Tracie Wendorf-Salgado

It was a Monday. But it wasn't an ordinary Monday; it was also the first day of summer break. I had been looking forward to a break after a long year of teaching middle schoolers who are deaf and hard of hearing. They had also informed me I was being laid off because there weren't enough students to justify my position. No problem. I knew God had it under control.

I had spent the weekend setting up and racing in a local triathlon. It was an Olympic-distance race, and I had finished in my usual middle-of-the-pack place. Sunday had been a great day.

But now it was Monday, just before 8:00 AM. I was driving down Highway 16 in town with my son and our family dog. Since it was around the time people needed to get to work, the road was busy. It was a three-lane highway running north and south. Three lanes, each direction. We were in the far-left lane. That's important to know.

My son, John, was eight. We were on our way to the eye doctor for an appointment for him. His teacher had expressed concern just before school ended that he was having issues in reading, not being able to see words correctly. We had been to an ophthalmologist, but she had some concerns and sent us to a specialist, someone who works specifically with children's vision issues. But that's really neither here nor there. What's important is that despite my son being only eight, he kept his wits in a very dangerous and scary situation.

We were driving down the highway on our way to the appointment. It was Monday-morning busy. Like I mentioned, we were in the far-left lane of three lanes. Suddenly, I couldn't breathe. I didn't know what was happening. My chest. It hurt, but not in a painful way. It was like someone was inside my trachea and slowly pinching it, but then letting it go. A pinching pain, and without breath.

The last thing I remember before seeing the firefighter, was grabbing my cell phone, tossing it in the back seat to my son, and saying, "Call—" My eight-year-old son later told me I slumped over into the passenger seat and the car slowly made its way through rush-hour traffic before somehow coming to an easy stop along the curb in the right-hand turn lane. We went from the far-left lane and crossed three lanes of traffic to stop in the right-hand turn lane. To this day, I have no idea how it happened in the kind of traffic we were in that morning. It still makes me shake my head in wonderment.

I say it was an angel.

Suddenly, there was a firefighter rapping on my window. I slowly picked up my head and looked around, wondering what the sound was, who he was, where I was. What happened?

He rapped again, "Ma'am! Ma'am, are you okay? Open your window, please." I saw the bumper of a semi fly by.

Slowly, I sat up. I heard my son in the back, "Mommy. Mommy, I thought you died. Mommy."

I looked around, still so confused. I did not know what was happening. Time seemed to go in reverse. It was so slow. Words were garbled, voices were hard to understand, everything was so bright.

"Ma'am. I need you to open your window, please. Now, please."

I pushed the button, and the window went down. I went out again.

When I came to again, I was sitting on the curb and the firefighter was next to me. He was forcing me to take a pill of some kind, baby aspirin, I learned later. He thought I was having a heart attack. No, not a heart attack, kind sir. Turns out, my heart started to randomly stop beating. Today was the first of many.

I went out again, this time slumping against him. This time was a little shorter. When I came to, I was in the ambulance. My then-husband was standing there, holding our son's hand. John's eyes were as big as the moon, and he was pale. My husband was telling them, with a tone of voice I've never heard—fear—which hospital to take me to, and they would meet the ambulance there.

I'm not going into the details of the hospital. What's really important here is that some random angel saved our lives. I was driving 60 miles an hour down a crowded highway on a rush-hour Monday morning when I passed out because my heart stopped beating. Even though I felt "funny" and was able to toss my phone to my son, he knew what to do. A child kept his wits and dialed his dad. All the while thinking I was dead. We're not sure who called 911. I truly believe it was the beautiful angel who so gently steered our car across three lanes of traffic to a safe spot so my baby wouldn't be injured.

"Mommy. Mommy, I thought you died. Mommy."

I will never forget his little boy voice saying that to me. It's seared into my heart. He said it with absolute quiet emotion. Fear. Confidence. Fear. My normally vivacious, loud, bouncy little boy sat in his car seat in the backseat, his voice filled with fear and scarily quiet.

"Mommy. Mommy, I thought you died. Mommy."

Thank you to the angel who was with us that Monday morning. I'm eternally grateful for two lives being saved that day.

Tracie and her son, John, dancing at his wedding.

Tracie Wendorf-Salgado is a 53-year-old mom to three beautiful adult children, a wife, and a teacher. Raised in Germantown, WI, she moved to Arizona four years ago to escape the brutal upper-Midwest winters. Tracie has High Grade AV Block, Intermittent, Type III managed with a pacemaker. But it doesn't stop her from doing anything—she's done five Ironman races, four with her pacemaker. She and her now-husband run and bike long distances in the mountains of Arizona, hike to the bottom of Grand Canyon, and explore all the back miles of the lone desert. To cool off, she enjoys a long swim at Lake Pleasant.

CHAPTER 7

FACING MY MORTALITY

Perhaps unsurprisingly, this intro was the hardest for me to write. Even now, as I am sitting captive on a train, I am struggling with the elephant in the (heart) chamber. So often, we are celebrated as resilient, brave and strong, that it's hard to acknowledge that we might feel the opposite. Like many of you, I have had brushes with my mortality, and it's never not frightening.

I lay in my little white bed in coronary care, my heart rate at 170, again. These episodes were becoming a familiar occurrence, to the point where they bored me. A commercial break in life, waiting in line for the roller coaster. Yawn. At least this ward had free television.

My nurse for that evening was a friendly middle-aged man, we'll call him Gordon, who enjoyed chatting. I was happy to pass the time waiting for the CHD specialist to prescribe an infusion of a notorious anti-arrhythmic so I could get out of there.

Gordon looked at the game show I was watching and pointed to one of the contestants. "I remember that man. He used to have a TV show where he pranked people. Then somebody was killed, and he could never bring himself to work on TV again."

After dinner, my family came to visit, and thankfully, so did the doctors. They attached the bag of medicine to my IV. I cannot explain, but like Han

Solo, I had a bad feeling about this. "Could you just stay?" I said to my husband and Gordon.

Within seconds, I felt cold, like a venomous snake had bitten me. So far, so good. Then I felt nauseous. Uh oh. I breathed out and inhaled what felt like wet cement. And stopped breathing. I looked across and glimpsed my heart and oxygen saturation rates dropping rapidly. Everything turned to melting stained glass. The last thing I saw was Gordon pushing the emergency button. 'I'm going to feel bad for him if I die.' Two white blobs appeared and pulled the brown blob that was my husband, in his winter coat, out of the room. Then a white blob pulled the IV out of my arm and put a bag of oxygen on me, and I started to breathe again.

To this day, I have no idea why that happened. My lungs crackled for weeks, and I scheduled a much-needed ablation to get off some of my medication. Mentally, it was rough. That day had started off great—it was a beautiful sunny day, and I took the dogs to the park. Then at around 8:00 p.m. I was almost dead. The thought that I would have to go back to work seemed absurd. Could you imagine Rambo working in an office?

Somehow, I did fine for a few years, then cracks started to appear in my early 30s. I remember doing things like going to work in my pyjamas and getting dressed when I got there, or breaking down in the car park in a shopping centre, which is especially embarrassing when you don't have a car. Those incidents and more prompted me to see a psychologist, which was a helpful start. My experience is just one of many. Mental health problems are something many of us face, whether it's trauma from medical and other adverse experiences, underlying neurodevelopmental conditions, or just our genes twisting the knife that bit more and giving us a side of psychosis with our cyanosis (sorry, I couldn't help myself).

This chapter will be a hard read, but I feel it's important to witness the raw honesty of the authors as they describe the role mortality played in their lives. David Franco's adult life was just beginning when he had a stroke during a valve replacement surgery, forcing him to adapt to a new normal. Margaret Raymond talks about her personal experiences of trauma, the impact it had on her development growing up and receiving care as an adult, and how she cares for her mental health. Becca Atherton's pieces, 'Car Ride Home' and 'You Can't Even Imagine' perfectly capture the desolation and anticipatory grief of losing control of one's body and life and having to face the prospect of dying young. Travis Martin's essay is about how he found his way back to a healthy lifestyle after years of partying in college left him overweight and facing a kidney transplant. His essay shows that even though having CHD is beyond our control, we have the power to make decisions about our lifestyle that can improve our health. Lauren Elizabeth's poem 'Clear' is about the power of faith when facing medical crises. Leslie Castro-Duitman's 'Dear Heart' is a farewell to the heart she was born with, written in the hours prior to her heart transplant. Finally, Michael Montgomery's piece describes the visceral experience of being in the operating theatre prior to being put under for surgery, an experience which was exceptionally jarring for him as his CHD had made itself known earlier that day on the football field. Thank you for reading this chapter, which brings the "shadow" CHD casts on us into the light.

It's Not Just the Age, It's the Mileage

by David Franco

"I can't see!" Terror gripped me as I opened my eyes, but couldn't see anything beyond flashing points of light.

What was worse than that was that nobody believed me. I sank back on the bed. How in the world did I get here?

Just a little over two months earlier, I had gotten married. It was a great time in my life. Working at the Texas Lottery was a challenging job that meant I had health insurance and other great benefits. As a hotline supervisor for the brand-new lottery program, I had learned enough to be sent to Atlanta to help Georgia set up its own lottery.

One day after work, I hopped in my car and headed to yet another cardiology appointment. The cardiologist put his icy stethoscope on my chest and listened intently. Saying little, he moved around and put it on my back. "Take a deep breath," he instructed me. "David," the cardiologist had said, "I think it's time, but let's do a transesophageal echo to make sure. I'm hearing a whooshing sound that makes me concerned about your pulmonary valve."

At 27 years of age, it was almost inevitable. I was born with a complex heart condition called 'congenitally-corrected transposition of the great arteries' or ccTGA for short. I had only had one open-heart surgery, but by 27 years of age, I figured I was due.

In my younger days, things were different. At that time, patients smoked in their hospital beds. Even though I was a kid, I was almost always on an adult floor where all the heart patients received care.

Rooms had windows you could open, and everything had that hospital smell—stale cigarette smell mixed with disinfectant that smelled more like an 'infectant.'

"It's time to replace your pacemaker!" Those were words spoken to me over and over again, making the hospital my home-away-from home.

At 27 years of age, I was able to make decisions for my healthcare myself. "I know where I need to go," I informed the cardiologist. There was no doubt in my mind. My first open-heart surgery was done in 1972 in Alabama and the assistant surgeon for that surgery was now the surgeon who would do my procedure.

I passed pumpkins, ghosts, and mock tombstones as I drove to the hospital. A few hospital employees were dressed up in costumes. "Son, did yuh bring yuh blue suede shoes with yuh?" An Elvis impersonator asked me as I signed into the hospital.

I just smiled and thought back to the conversation I had had with my new bride. "Don't worry!" I assured her. "I've been down this road before. It's not my first rodeo."

Pam looked at me, wide-eyed with concern. "Do you need me to go with you?"

"I've been through all of this before," I remember telling her. "Look, it's pretty simple. They're going to take out my pulmonary valve and replace it with a porcine or pig valve. The whole surgery should be six hours, tops. I'll probably be there for 10 days and then I'll be home again. Good as new! No! Better than new because I'll have a brand-new pacemaker inserted, too! Mom is going to meet me at the hospital. We've got this."

Preliminary tests were done. They admitted me to the hospital. Everything was going according to plan. Until it wasn't.

They deemed my heart surgery a success. Mom wasn't allowed in the Cardiac ICU. "We're having a little trouble waking David up," she was told. Although not comatose, I couldn't seem to wake up.

I don't remember any of that. I felt the stiff hospital sheets on my body and my brain groggily remembered where I was. "Wake up," I said to myself. I could hear the machines hooked up to me making their typical noises. My bed was near the window and I could feel the heat of the sun falling on me, but when I opened my eyes . . . nothing. My tongue felt too big for my mouth and I could hardly speak. "I can't see!" I wanted to shout. In response, I struggled and pulled out all the IVs, the EKG electrodes popped off as I struggled against the sheets and blanket. 'I need to get out of here,' I thought. 'I want to go home!'

"It's okay, David," Mom was saying while she and the nurse tried to restrain me. "David, stop!" Mom begged me.

Time had no meaning while I blindly clung to the hope that my sight would return. Closing my eyes, I couldn't believe this was happening to me. In the quiet of the night, I could feel my mother's presence and knew she would be saying a rosary for me. I knew God was with me, but I felt forsaken at that dreadful time.

"Mom," I said hoarsely, "I see dancing lights."

"Pam, you need to get here now," Mom said to my new wife from a telephone in the hallway.

Nurses changed shifts, doctors came and went. Finally, my wife and my mother were by my side.

"What's your name?" "What year is it?"

"Who's the president of the United States?"

I answered in a slurry and shaking voice, "David Franco, the year is 1958 and the President is Dwight Eisenhower." The year was wrong, but I knew who the President was in 1958.

"He's having trouble with his entire right side," said the nurse to a doctor. "I think he's had a stroke."

"Mom, where's Pam?" I remember asking.

"I'm here," she said, but I couldn't see her until she was directly in front of me. I felt so alone. Would I ever feel like myself again?

"We're going to order a series of tests," the doctor informed us. "We need a spinal tap, an electroencephalogram (EEG), and a head CAT scan."

"There's nothing really wrong with David," the neurologist said. "His brain activity is a little slow, but otherwise, I can't find anything wrong."

"Where is the cardiologist?" Pam asked.

"He had to go to a conference after David's surgery," Mom replied.

I sank into the bed feeling more alone than I ever remember feeling. I couldn't see. I could barely move. I knew my speech was slurred. 'I've had a stroke,' I thought to myself. 'Nurse Farrell is right. Why won't anyone listen to us?'

"He's just having an adverse reaction to the anesthesia," I overheard someone saying.

"I think he's a malingerer," a cardiologist said. I knew what they were saying and thinking. They thought I didn't want to recover. Were they crazy?

"How many more tests are you going to give him?" Pam asked after I'd already failed the strength test, the cognitive test, the coordination test, and the gait test.

"We can't figure out what's wrong," she was told.

"Let's go ahead and replace your pacemaker," a doctor said about a week after my valve surgery. How can time move at a snail's pace and yet go by so quickly?

"It's finally time to go home!" Pam informed me. It had been three weeks, not the 10 days I had prepared her for.

"You'll get cardiac rehab at home, David," Mom said. "You're going to get better."

"David, we believe you've had a stroke and we're going to do everything we can to help you," I was told at rehab. They saved my life in so many ways. Occupational therapy, speech therapy, physical therapy and visual therapy all focused on getting me back to who I was before they replaced the valve. It was the cognitive therapy that was the biggest lingering problem after the stroke.

"I can't play the guitar," I said to Mom on the phone one day. "My right hand just doesn't want to do what I know it can do."

Relearning how to play the guitar became one therapy that helped me find myself again. I find it is the small things that seem to bother me in

life. I'm so upset at all my losses and changes in capabilities; however, I'm still very much alive. I became a different person in so many ways.

"I don't know what I would have done without you," I said to Dr. Harris, the man who diagnosed my stroke. "Without you and my cognitive therapist, Ruthann Curtis, I wouldn't be where I am today." He brushed aside my praise, but I'm introspective. I realize I probably wouldn't still be married to my wife of 25 years. I doubt I would be able to drive, play the guitar, or raise my daughter into adulthood. Looking back on everything that has happened to me in my life, I realize that it's not the years we live that matter, it's what we do with the time we have. I've learned to appreciate my daughter's laughter, the warm Texas sunshine on my back when I'm barbecuing, jamming on my guitar or even sitting alone with my cat Thomas while we work together on my computer. Additionally, there's the joy of witnessing another Corpus Christi sunset with my dog Douglas and my daughter, Sarah, after visiting her at college, following yet another cardiology appointment.

David Franco was born on December 19, 1966. He grew up in Hastings-on-Hudson, New York. David was father to Sarah, and he was a very hands-on, stay-at-home dad. He was a fur father to his cat Thomas and his dog Douglas. David was also a co-host for the podcast Heart to Heart with Nicole and David *and he volunteered with Hearts Unite the Globe as a sound engineer, a producer, and wherever else he was needed. David was a devout Catholic, and he was an accomplished guitarist. He often took his guitar to CHD conferences, where he would jam with anyone willing. He was a big CHD activist, and he took part in various fundraising projects to raise money and awareness of CHDs.*

Editor's Note: *Sadly, David passed away on March 12, 2020 from complications related to his CHD. He was in the dog park with his constant companion, Douglas, by his side.*

Car Ride Home

by Becca Atherton

My head was pressed against the cold car window as I watched the world blur together. My head was pounding, probably from the sinus infection. But the fears that were crammed into my mind didn't help any. "Your lung function is down 20 percent . . . " I squeezed my eyes shut, trying to forget what Dr. Conrad (a pulmonologist) had said so plainly. She may be used to this information, but my family and I weren't comfortable with this.

I leaned back from the window to look more directly at my reflection. 'God, Becca, pull yourself together,' I scolded myself as I wiped my eyes with the back of my hand. I had calmed myself down before I could cry when the news was told to me, but now my face was dripping wet. "Looking like we are moving closer to the transplant," Dr. Conrad's voice echoed. I sniffled quietly. I don't want my parents to know just now how scared I really am.

Fear . . . one of the scariest feelings in the world. There was no way around it. Once fear gets inside of you, it eats away at you. Fear becomes a part of you.

Moving closer to transplant . . . I shivered as the words came back to mind. I clenched my iPod, wishing the music could drown my fears. I searched through my library, trying to find a happy song, hoping that would help. It didn't. I was too wrapped up with the idea of needing a transplant that I couldn't even hear the song.

I pressed my small forehead up against the window again. I stared at my reflection, thinking I looked like an idiot with my nose scrunched against the glass. An enormous sigh escaped my lips, making a light frost set on the window. I broke away to look at the frost and I drew a heart in the middle with my finger. Then, mad at my heart, I wiped all the frost off with my sleeve.

I pressed my hand to the window, feeling the coldness of the glass on my palm. I felt something small and wet roll down my face. I wiped my eyes with the back of my hand, but that didn't stop the salty tears from dripping onto my lips. I kicked the back of my mom's seat, trying to get my anger out. "You okay?" my mom inquired, feeling the kick on the back of her chair. I started nodding my head, but then quickly changed to shaking. I couldn't keep it in any longer. I let my head fall into my hands and I sobbed.

"Boo, what's wrong?" my mom asked, taking my hand in hers. She didn't need an explanation, though. She already knew.

"I don't want to die…" I choked out, head still in my hands.

My mom gave my knee a gentle pat before speaking calmly, "I don't want you to die either, Boo."

I already knew that, but what I wanted her to do was promise me I wouldn't die. Not now, not later, not ever. "Promise me, Mom. Promise me that I won't die." I begged her, lifting my head from my hands to look her in the eyes.

"We are trying Boo, we're trying. I can't promise, but we are trying."

A note from Chris Atherton, Becca's Mom:

Becca had dreams . . . She loved life,

She loved people.

She was afraid she would be forgotten . . .

Please hold her close . . .

when you graduate, start a new job, hang out with family, try a new recipe, go to heart camp, share a low-salt option, get married, welcome children, stand up for those being excluded, need strength, ride a thrilling rollercoaster, give a speech, remember with your siblings, volunteer your time, grow old, listen to someone who is hurting . . .

Please let Becca walk beside you to share in your joy.

Please help her, through you, to continue to make a difference.

Becca—Forever Loved, Forever Missed, Forever 26 (10/09/1992-10/12/2018)

Free-Falling

by Margaret Raymond

I was playing in a sandbox, one not big enough to sit in, but large enough that I could bury the therapist's toys in it. The wooden dolls with bendy arms and legs were a favorite, since similar ones were hogged by the popular kids at school. Sessions were often boring unless I initiated what we'd play. So that day, I buried the doll with the yellow braids.

"What happened to her, Margaret?" the therapist asked.

"She's dead."

I can recall the silence that followed because I experience it to this day when my brain spits out a truth I'm not ready to unpack. Eventually I realized what I had done and quickly dug the girl up, saying, "Ta-da! She's alive. See, look." I held her out for my therapist's inspection and waited for her to agree. She must have reacted in some manner, but what I recall is her bowing her head and writing furiously in her notebook.

My understanding of my life before the age of five comes from stories like these, shared by members of my family. Recalling anything before the age of five is like attempting to overcome my fear of needles: it's nearly impossible. I rely on these stories to gauge who I was during a time I've blocked out. My almost-superhero-like power to forget scary things, and the bright red scar from the tip of my sternum to the middle of my abdomen, were not what made me feel different. It was my ability to protect myself from hard truths that, when finally forced to face them, made me realize exactly *how* I was different.

I grew up too fast. Faced death too early. I wanted to know the *why* of life while trying to stay young. It was a strange combination: emotionally older because of the medical trauma, yet purposefully attempting to regress in academics. It was my way of trying to stay young when the world forced me to grow up.

I didn't have a near-death experience, so I can't say for sure why I was preoccupied with the meaning of life and what happens after you die, but I was.

I am.

We look for answers from the people who care for us, but when their answer to the what-happens-when-we-die question is, "Well, do you remember what it was like before you were born?", it makes you feel like you're free-falling.

I'm in my late twenties and I often feel like I've jumped out of a plane with no parachute. I hate this feeling with a passion, but no one, not even the best therapists in the world, could have fully prepared me for every moment I'm to feel uncertain or uncomfortable. That's what I've learned anxiety is: uncertainty and uncomfortableness. With this knowledge, I've at least been able to identify which one I'm feeling and take steps to calm myself down.

For example: today I had an MRI with a contrast solution, consequently . . . needles. I've been anxious for the last four days. My anxiety has led to jitters, stomach upset, and enhanced sense of smell (yes, this one is strange, but it happens to me). So, what do I do about it? I share my fear with the medical professional. So, after I assured the Magnetic Resonance Imaging (MRI) technician that, no, I wasn't going to pass out, and that yes, I probably would cry my eyes out, he said, "I could just give you numbing cream."

Excuse me?

Can you tell I'm slightly annoyed at having paid therapists to tell me none of this?

Numbing cream, apparently, is commonly given to patients who have a needle phobia. So while therapists were going off about costly exposure therapy options, there was always a prescription tube of numbing cream that I could not only request at medical procedures, but that I could buy at the pharmacy.

I said, "Numb me up!"

Ten minutes later, the IV was in and I was crying. Even though I felt nothing except his hand on my arm, it had triggered me.

That's the strange thing about trauma. It doesn't ever really go away. It's just like my heart will never have normal anatomy. I will always have tricuspid atresia (TA). Even if I get a transplant, I'll consider myself a TA survivor because the condition doesn't make me who I am. My experiences do. My ability to endure does.

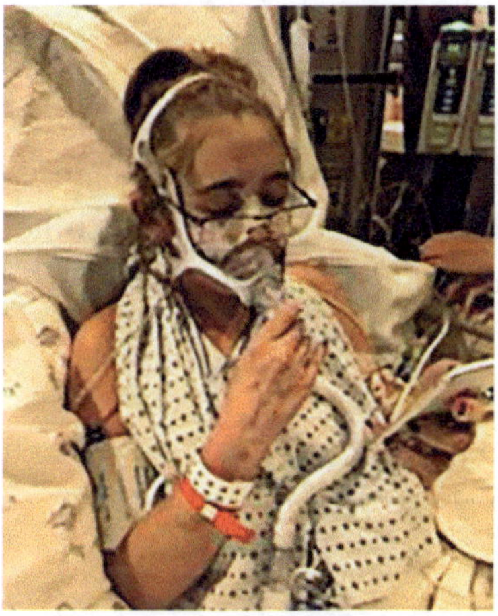

Enduring, however, is not necessarily living. For me, enduring is living moment to moment. That is the coping mechanism I developed to handle the unscheduled visits of an Indian phlebotomist and the nurses with sympathetic smiles and freezing hands. That coping mechanism served me well, really well, except for when I was ready to stop fearing the future. I've learned that living in the moment means holding your anxiety for what's to come at arm's length. And as I get older and my health starts to change, I know my coping strategy needs to as well. I've sought therapists, attempted meditation and yoga, except it did nothing but force me into my old coping strategy: staying in the moment. I needed the opposite, like exposure therapy to the future.

What worked? Besides realizing the medical community had held out on me, I stumbled upon a therapist who had an answer no one else in her profession had thought to share. Of all places to meet her: a professional development day at work. She spoke about anxiety, how it is ruled by uncomfortableness and uncertainty.

This was the missing link I needed to recognize, that life is passive without moments of uncomfortableness and uncertainty. What makes life active, or in my brain 'worth living,' is overcoming those moments instead of pushing them away or trying to forget. Living moment to moment, without preparing for the future, was enabling my anxiety to control how I live. I'd been attempting to perpetually be comfortable and certain. Living doesn't guarantee either. Once that clicked, my anxiety lessened. Did it fix it? No. Have I completely overcome my trauma? No, although it may lessen with time, I don't think I will ever be rid of it. I'm still the little girl trying to make sense of death, trying to uncover all the dolls in the sand.

Trying is ultimately the difference between living a life passively or actively. I'll make mistakes. I'll resist change. I'll fall into old habits, hide myself in the comfortableness of certainty. This cycle may continue, except now I have the knowledge to recognize the pattern and the motivation to pick up the shovel and dig myself out.

Margaret Ellis Raymond is a freelance developmental editor who believes everyone has a story and unique voice. She was born with tricuspid atresia and shares her medical journey on YouTube under the channel name Unbeatable. *Her hobbies include photography, saving the monarch butterflies, and a daily habit of laughing too much. She currently lives in the beautiful state of Maine.*

You Can't Even Imagine

by Becca Atherton

You can't even imagine
What it feels like
To know you are dying
You can't even imagine
What it feels like
To look at your parents
Knowing you may never see them again
Or how it feels to look around a room bursting with loneliness
And know that this place
This frightening place
May be the last thing you see before you die
You can't even imagine
The horrifying embarrassment of having to ask your mom to help you to the bathroom
At age 13, your strength is too fragile for you to even undo your own hospital gown
It feels as if you are back at age two
With your mom guiding you onto the freezing porcelain toilet, then back down
Your dignity is stolen away from you because of your own body
You can't even imagine
Looking at yourself in the bathroom mirror
And seeing yourself for what might be the last time

The last time you see yourself and all you can see is your sunken eyes of sickness

The paper white complexion of a malicious infection eating its way through your body

Slowly swimming through your fragile veins and into your bloodstream,

You can't even imagine

The sadness that consumes not only your mind,

But every inch of your trembling body

When you see for the first time in weeks,

Just how sick you truly are

You can't even imagine

The terror

Of having your life placed into the hands of someone else

You can't even imagine

The fear that overwhelms you when the mask is placed over your face

The plastic smell of medicine consumes your lungs

And you plead, "Please don't let me die."

You know you are no longer in control of your life

You can't even imagine

What it feels like

To know you may never wake up

From not only surgery

But also from this all too real nightmare

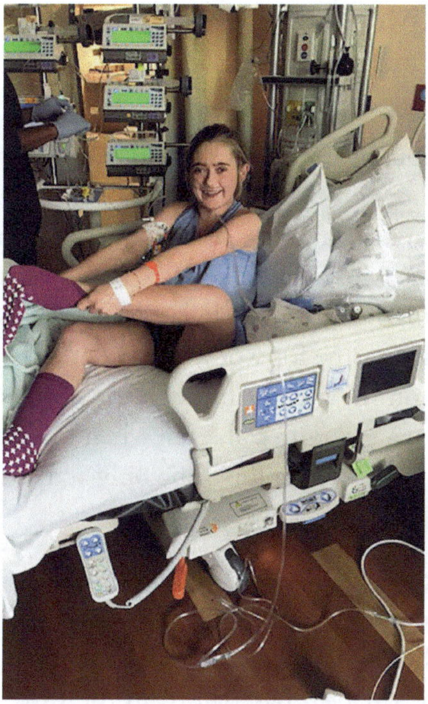

Becca Atherton was bright, beautiful, inclusive, kind, caring and brave, with a little bit of sass. She was a public speaker and an advocate for anti-bullying and congenital heart defect awareness. Becca has a blog where she shared her CHD journey. She was a Yelp Elite Food Critic with an emphasis on low salt options. Becca was fluent in American Sign Language. She was a mentor and an inspiration to many.

"She made broken look beautiful and strong look invincible. She walked with the Universe on her shoulders and made it look like a pair of wings." —Ariana Dancu

Becca—Forever Loved, Forever Missed, Forever 26 (10/09/1992-10/12/2018)

New Diet, New Life

by Travis Martin

Life was good. I thought nothing would ever go wrong. Unfortunately, that is not always how life works. In 2013, I ended up in the hospital, dehydrated and in renal failure. This was just after my second year of college. The previous two years looked like a scene out of *Animal House.* I was drinking regularly, living off dollar menus and sleeping as little as possible. I was making time for work, school, and the fraternity life and my health was not on my radar. Although the hospitalization was scary, it was not enough of a wake-up call, even when I heard the doctor in the hospital say my kidneys were failing. The only actual change I made was that I started seeing a nephrologist.

My childhood was unbelievably normal, after being born with an atrioventricular septal defect and a hypoplastic left ventricle. In March 1993, I received the gift of life in a heart transplant and thrived from that point forward. I played baseball from the time I could stand and got my black belt in Tae Kwon Do by the age of 8. It was a shock to most people to learn of my transplant, seeing the accomplishments and success I had as a kid. As time went on, I kept the information to myself to reduce the coddling and worry people felt after learning I had a 'condition.' I was told often that I was just as healthy, if not healthier, than most kids my age.

As 2014 started, the partying slowed down, but my diet seemed to take a serious downturn. I wasn't facing any immediate health challenges, but I started gaining weight and eventually hit my heaviest point in my life. My kidney function remained low, but I was only being told that there was a problem without being given any ways to repair the situation. There was a disconnect that made me feel like I was completely doomed, and the only way to improve things would be with medication and an eventual kidney transplant.

In May 2015, I was with a close friend of mine, a vegan and lover of all things holistic. We spent most of our time watching documentaries and playing Mario Kart (usually unproductive), but on this day, I experienced a paradigm shift—one that would ultimately change my life and the trajectory of my health. We checked out a new documentary titled *Fed Up*, an explanation through storytelling of the negative impact of sugar consumption in processed food and most products we enjoy on a day-to-day basis. I was shocked. The simplistic breakdown of the problem resonated with me as I left her house after the film. I went straight home and watched another film, *Fat, Sick and Nearly Dead*, about an Aussie that came to America to complete a 60-day juice cleanse.

In just three scant hours, my entire perception of food and diet had changed. It was as if a freight train had run me over, then backed up to make sure I got the point. I went into my kitchen and threw away everything that didn't align with my new beliefs, which was pretty much everything I had. The next day was Cinco de Mayo. I woke up and found a juice place near my house and began my journey as a vegan. Over the next two months, I juiced two to three times a day and only usually ate one meal a day. To be perfectly honest, the lack of meals resulted from my lack of cooking awareness or what I could eat to fit my alternative lifestyle. Looking back, it makes perfect sense I lost 40 pounds in two months. I was basically only taking in liquids.

Right around this two-month mark, I went to get labs done to see if the change was more than just weight loss. I received a call a couple of days later, requesting that I go back in for labs because the results appeared to be wrong. A few days after the second draw, I dropped by the nephrologist's office to see how everything was looking. Her eyes widened when she saw me. I looked healthier, more vibrant, and leaner than I had at any point before this. When I told my doctor I was living a vegan lifestyle, she leapt out of her chair and hugged me in excitement. Turns out, the labs were correct and this change in lifestyle had a profound effect on my kidneys, returning them to nearly normal function for the first time in almost a decade.

It seemed that this may be an answer to prolonging my life and improving my overall health. As the months progressed, I got into a groove and learned how to eat properly, while still juicing every day. My diet has been extremely clean, but at times I have fallen a bit short. The one thing that has stayed consistent is the lack of animal proteins.

The last four years have had moments of strong dedication and absolute uncertainty. Ultimately, though, this change has motivated me to continue to research and listen to what my body needs on the path to becoming the healthiest version of myself. As my health has improved and brought me amazing results, my desire to help people has become a passion. I enjoy sharing my story to motivate and encourage others. I am now happily married and have resumed living the 'normal' life I had throughout my childhood.

Travis with his daughter Ellie

Travis with his wife Pamela and daughter Ellie

Travis Martin continued to work on educating others on using nutrition to live a healthier life. He also worked with a local not-for-profit with Transplant Families, helping to educate them on making the most of their second chance at life. Travis and his wife Pamela had a baby girl, Ellie, in July 2021. Travis experienced a severe transplant rejection episode of his heart in August 2021. The pandemic had taken a toll on the monitoring of his health. The rejection was being managed, and he was improving, although facing a future re-transplant. Unfortunately, he did not get the opportunity for that second transplant, as he contracted chicken pox in January 2022. Chicken pox is dangerous in the immunocompromised and in just one short week, it took his life.

Editor's Note: *Special thanks to Dawn Martin for helping to edit Travis' contribution after he passed away. Our condolences to the family and all who loved Travis.*

Clear

by Lauren Elizabeth

I never know when it will come, how long it will stay, or even if it will ever go away.

It always takes me by surprise. There's no rhyme or reason to its ways.

I try not to panic, to stay calm, but soon I find fear approaches on.

I take slow, deep breaths, but my breath feels so weak and my heart leaps in me as the palpitations make me dizzy.

I feel it beat in my throat, my chest tightens, and my heart feels squeezed by a rope.

Feeling faint, thoughts run wild through my head as I reflect on death.

Fear leaves as I pray and I am reminded that I am not in control of today.

Not today, not tomorrow, for the Lord is in sovereign control and even me, He holds.

The sirens are loud; doctors are all around, unfamiliar with my condition.

When fear creeps in again, I am reminded of their position.

They are just instruments in His hand and He is the ultimate I AM.

The pain is real. I can't think straight, but He keeps me sane.

Small, silent prayers of truth draw me near and are all I can manage to cling to.

The night seems long as hours pass on, but what precious time I pray I do not waste.

I want my actions and words to reflect His name, even amid lasting pain.

Finally, the time comes, and the Lord gives me peace as the doctors put me to sleep.

Fading away fast, a few tears run down my cheek as I have conflicting feelings about the evening.

The question arrives in my mind; 'Will I awaken this time?' *To live is Christ, to die is gain* is what I hold to as I fade away.

Clear. I first hear the noises as I slowly open my eyes and look around.

I utter a prayer thanking the Lord for awaking me to another day. My heart feels normal; the pain is gone, yet exhaustion draws on.

At a young age, doctors restructured my heart that was missing the left part.

My heart surgery caused rhythm issues, due to scar tissue.

Supraventricular tachycardia is the name for your heart beating like it's insane.

But, what beauty there is in being physically reminded that every heartbeat is in His hand and that which seems unplanned is in fact actually under His command.

I ask myself, 'Where are my priorities? Am I serving the One in all Authority?'

I don't want to waste my life, for this time is fleeting and every day He gives me is a blessing.

To the cross I must cling. In the Spirit I must abide. In Jesus I must hide, every day until eternity. For on that day when you finally don't awaken and you get to meet your maker, what a waste it would be to say, "I lived for the finite things."

Lauren Elizabeth was born in Texas on January 27, 1992, with hypoplastic left heart syndrome (HLHS) and transposition of the great arteries (TGA). At 18 months old, she underwent the Fontan surgery and was given a pacemaker that she no longer relies on. In high school, she developed arrhythmia problems due to scar tissue on her heart, which began the start of her battle with arrhythmia. Over the years, Lauren has experienced a few different types of arrhythmias and has gone through good seasons and hard seasons, but one thing always remains the same: her faith in Jesus being with her every step of the way. In her free time, Lauren enjoys playing guitar, writing, and serving her local church. Lauren is currently working on a memoir that she plans to release in 2024.

Dear Heart

by Leslie Castro-Duitman

This poem is one depiction of how a dying person sees her heart before transplantation. The poem also provides an insight of how poorly one's cognitive skills slowly decline in the writing process before transplantation. Misspelled words, omission of words, scrambled words, thinking I have made a masterpiece, but in actuality it's all a blob on paper. All because of the decline in heart and the lack of oxygenated blood flow running through the body.

Dear Heart,

We've fought so many battles together, from birth until now,

You've seen me at the worst and you've seen me at my best.

Too bad you couldn't stick around, but it's truly your time to go.

Today is the day like any others, it's ups and downs, it's highs and lows,

But of all days, your last days, your last hours, your last seconds.

So I just want to say thank you,

Thank you for keeping my heart beating.

Thank you for the first few beats of life.

Thank you for pulling through our first surgery . . . (Blalock-Taussig Shunt), who knew that we would pull through it.

Thank you for all the cardiac caths, most of which a small statured man managed to do.

Thank for you for the second surgery, they say it was called the Fontan procedure.

Thank you for not failing me, even though you tried to on one too many attempts.

Thank you for the third surgery, even though I had my doubts and fears.

You always managed to pull through time and time again.

Now I must say to you, goodbye.

Good bye for everything.

You were my friend, you were my foe.

You were the happiness in me, you were the sad in me.

You were as strong as a rock, you were as weak as a mouse.

You were the hatred, anger, frustration, hopelessness, and fear.

You were the part me that I love, you were the parts of me I hated.

You were my one and only first true love . . .

My heart . . .

May you Rest In Peace!

Thank you for everything!!!

(4-18-73 to 8-08-19)

RIP

Leslie Castro-Duitman

When you're facing the brink of death, the realization of having the surgeon remove an organ from your body and replacing your organ with someone else's organ is mind-boggling and difficult to process. At least, the process was arduous for me, so I wrote this poem literally hours before my heart transplant in 2019.

A special thanks to the cardiac surgeon, Dr. Christopher Sciortino, the hepatitis C coordinator, Traci Snyder-Mcgaha, and the cardiac transplant team at Presbyterian Hospital in Pittsburgh and my family.

and

A special thanks to my 29-year-old female, intravenous drug addict organ donor who helped prolong my life so that I may live to tell my story.

Leslie Castro is a congenital heart disease survivor who was diagnosed in 1973 at four months old with tricuspid atresia, pulmonary stenosis, and multiple other congenital heart defects. In 1985, Leslie successfully had the Fontan procedure at 12. When Leslie was 31 years old, she had the Fontan procedure, Cox Maze III procedure and pacemaker implantation. In 2019, Leslie willingly accepted a hepatitis C heart donor organ from a 29-year-old female intravenous drug user.

Even though Leslie grew up with congenital heart disease, it didn't stop her from becoming an elementary teacher or receiving a master's degree in education. She has traveled extensively throughout the United States, Canada, Mexico, Caribbean, Central America, Europe, and Africa. She's bilingual in English and in Spanish and she loves traveling, hiking, reading, photography, and exercising.

Leslie has been an advocate for CHD since 2006, advocating with the Adult Congenital Heart Disease Association and Conquering CHD.

A Heartbeat Away From Destiny

by Michael Montgomery

Lying in the operating room with IVs in my hand and an oxygen mask over my face, I could hear the nurses running around in preparation and the monitors beeping. My heartbeat was racing, and I was starting to sweat. The lights were extremely bright, and I was shaking uncontrollably. Maybe it was that it was strikingly cold in the operating room, or possibly me being so anxious. I was more nervous than I had ever been in my life up to that date and quite possibly, even since.

I was only a junior in college, but my heart was failing me. I worked so hard to achieve my dreams, only to fall short and land myself in a hospital and a few hours later to a disease I apparently had my whole life and didn't know.

Twenty-four hours earlier, on my first practice with Texas A&M, I fell to my knees out of breath with heart pain and passed out. They rushed me to the hospital where tests were done and concluded that I had a heart defect known as Wolff-Parkinson-White (WPW) disease. I needed emergency surgery—an ablation.

Everything I had worked for my whole life was contingent on how this operation succeeded. So many thoughts were racing through my mind while I took those deep breaths before surrendering to the anesthesia. I wondered, 'Are the doctors skilled enough to fix this? Would this condition create long-term problems? Would I have another heart attack? And most importantly to me, Would I ever be able to play football again?' I rebuked the fear and doubt and assured myself God hadn't brought me this far to fail me. I said a quiet prayer and fell asleep.

Michael Montgomery II is single and was born on August 18, 1983, to Pastor Michael Montgomery Sr. and Rosie Walker.

In high school, Michael earned All-State in football and basketball. He earned a full athletic scholarship to play football at Texas A&M. The Green Bay Packers drafted Michael (#96) and he played for five years in the NFL, and a year with UFL and CFL. They inducted him into the 2022 Navarro College Hall Of Fame.

When not with his dog, Optimus, you might see him on the big screen in films such as The Reason *or* Billy Lynn's Long Halftime Walk. *He also made guest appearances on network TV shows.*

As a near-death survivor, Michael works with charities and has founded The Heart of Michael nonprofit organization to promote awareness and to support aspiring youth athletes by facilitating access to heart screenings for communities across the country.

Transformation

Children often love to watch fuzzy caterpillars transform into beautiful butterflies. Some parents and teachers even buy butterfly kits to allow children to observe the life cycle of a butterfly up close. They see how the caterpillars grow and develop into beautiful butterflies and they also learn, if they're not careful, that without proper care, the caterpillars will die before achieving the butterfly state.

The transformation a caterpillar has to go through in order to become a butterfly is not unlike the transformation our heart warriors must endure to live beyond their congenital heart defect. Butterfly transformation is one of the most iconic transformations in nature. But what about the transformations our heart warriors go through?

In this book, you'll have a chance to read three different chapters in this section. The first chapter is entitled "Works of Art" and the chapter is abundant with poetry, art, and even some fiction. These works show the reader how having a CHD doesn't limit the imagination of our heart warriors. Just the opposite. Many in our community have extremely active imaginations and are able to capture moments in time with the stroke of a pen or a brush, or perhaps they capture a scene with just the right words, or create something magical simply with the beauty of their mind and descriptions that allow us to join them in their creation.

The second chapter honors our heart warrior authors. In this chapter, you will have a chance to read excerpts from their books and learn a little bit more about them, too. While 80% of people *want* to write a book, less than 2% of people actually publish. Our heart warriors beat the odds to survive and endure their CHDs. In this chapter, you'll witness how exceptional these heart warriors are since, once again, they have beaten the odds to become published authors.

The final chapter is entitled "Beyond My CHD" and it's the chapter that helps the reader to understand how heart defects may afflict our heart warriors, but they don't have to prevent our heart warriors from being the best versions of themselves. So many heart warriors have used their medical trauma as a springboard to metamorphose into exceptional individuals. "Post-traumatic growth" is the psychological term for these transformations. Those of us who believe in a higher being may feel they are more akin to miracles. Regardless what you call them, they are just as beautiful as the butterflies that fill our gardens in springtime.

CHAPTER 8

WORKS OF ART

When I put together the book *The Heart of a Father*, I reached out to some men whose wives wrote for *The Heart of a Mother*—partly because many of the contributors became close friends of mine over time, and because I thought readers might enjoy reading more about the families they met in *The Heart of a Mother*. Since I published the fathers' book 10 years later, readers saw how some of the heart warriors had grown up. It seemed logical that when I was finally putting together this book, I would reach out to those core families again. I knew that my devoted readers would want to know what happened to some of the heart warriors they had read about in a book published over 20 years earlier. Baby Hearts Press has actually been an important part of some families' legacies, and that is something we never could have guessed would happen when we put together our first books.

I felt a sense of loss when I realized that two of the women I felt sure would have wanted to contribute to this new book had passed away. I mentioned as much to both of their mothers and the mothers replied with copies of art their daughters had made. Therefore, this anthology has a special chapter highlighting the art of our heart warriors. Not all the contributors are deceased, but Karen Klein and Julie Kerr could be part of this book thanks to their mothers, and I'm thrilled about that. I'm sure everyone will enjoy Julie's cute ferret and her essay, and Karen's artwork, too.

My co-editor, Megan Tones, has written a piece called 'The Overworld,' previously published in *Masques*, which I'm sure you'll all want to read. My dear friend, Lisa Colvil, has included two of her poems ('Light of Love,' and 'Falling Apart') which I'm certain other CHDers will relate to, and which she first read on the *Heart to Heart with Anna* podcast. Becca Atherton sent me some heartfelt poems she wrote before she passed away. Because two of her poems dealt with facing her mortality, we felt it was more appropriate to include her poems in that chapter. Megan and I also felt that Becca Atherton's poem, 'I am a Miracle Child' really set the stage for all the essays to follow in the book; therefore, we put the poem just before the Dedication.

Ferret Artwork

by Julie Kerr

Julie applied a pointillism technique to this ferrets drawing for a high school art class assignment.

Julie and her ferret, Ellie

Julie was a mathematician who died at age 35. She got her first ferret at age 14 as a reward for undergoing two open-heart surgeries the previous year. She and her husband had 12 ferrets over the years, up to six at any one time. Julie's other interests were miniatures, vegan cooking, cello, community activism, and Esperanto.

Light of Love

by Lisa Colvil

All beautiful things
Are what the soul holds
In darkness, strength arises
The sky fills with hope
As the ray of light hits our hearts,
Always smile
For faith is
The light of love
Recognize the wonder of blessings
And never give up
The light of love
Will defeat the battles you face
For with every struggle
The end spells victory
For within us lives the light of love

Lisa Dang Colvil was born in Reading, Pennsylvania and raised in Garden Grove, California. She was born with ventricular septal defect (VSD), patent ductus arteriosus (PDA) with pulmonic stenosis, and double outlet right ventricle (DORV). She grew up loving reading and writing for fun. In 2019, Lisa became an author with her first book, Through the Beauty of Grace, I Will. *She met the heart community online in 2019/2020 and began her CHD journey. Lisa and her husband are parents to Serenity and Sean. Lisa's family also has a dog named Captain Morgan. The family moved into their first house in 2020. Lisa was born to Vietnamese refugee parents. She volunteers with The Heart Community Collection and Hearts Unite the Globe.*

Art

by Karen Klein

In addition to her work for Adult Congenital Heart Association (ACHA), Karen loved to paint. Seashells were one of her favorite subjects. Her parents, Mary Kay and Ted Klein, donated this seashell painting to the ACHA Office. In this photo, you can see Mary Kay and Ted flanking their daughter's artwork.

Karen was a co-founder and first President of the Adult Congenital Heart Association (ACHA), which was incorporated in 1998. Karen was born with Truncus Arteriosus Type III with an absent right pulmonary artery. Karen never had surgery for her CHD. In 2001, she married James McNulty, who had also been very involved with the ACHA since he was born with a single ventricle heart. In 2001, she married James McNulty, who had also been very involved with ACHA.

Sadly, Karen Klein McNulty died unexpectedly on August 31, 2005. Her husband James also left us on May 10, 2022.

Karen and husband James McNulty on their wedding day

Falling Apart

by Lisa Colvil

In the dark
When you are lost
Alone in the moments
You don't know if tomorrow is worth it
Life is never in one scene
Always moving
Always changing
Space and time
Falling apart
The trials are too strong
Don't know where to go
Falling apart
Only to be lifted up and comforted by the love
Of the Lord

Lisa Dang Colvil has been very busy writing in 2022. She published two additional devotionals, The Hope of a Heart Warrior *and* Whispers of Grace: Fall Through Winter Devotional. *She also started her Stardust Series, publishing two books so far. Lisa Dang Colvil's books are available for purchase on Amazon.com.*

Overworld

by Megan Tones

For the third song in a row, Elise stood entranced by the busker before her. The sound of passers by was muted by the narrow alley and his spell. He played something baroque on his violin and Elise thought she recognised it. Part of Vivaldi's Four Seasons perhaps. His left hand rolled over the changing octaves in perfect synch with the right, which mastered the bow with such speed that a heavy dust of resin mounted up on the strings, bridge and body. So well rehearsed that he needed no written notes to guide him, he was free to be in the thrall of the music—hopping up and down in a sort of jig when the music was merry, swaying when his fingers lilted into melancholia, and thrashing about when it approached metal. It was only when he started this strange dance that Elise noticed he had no shoes, though he wore well tailored black pants and a white shirt.

I'm not surprised he's busking then, she thought. He must be really poor if he can only afford half an outfit.

Engrossed as he was, the maestro was not without manners. He managed a tiny nod of acknowledgement at the occasional coin-dropper from the main thoroughfare, and Elise saw the way to his heart. She turned to her right and opened her small leather handbag. As she did so, a thick strand of hair dropped from her braid and over her left eye, Almost the same blonde as that horsehair bow, she thought.

From either side of the strand, she watched him watch her. She smiled at him and dropped one dollar. The violinist moved to another number, this time in a minor key. Elise dropped another dollar, and he added some harmonic improvisations. The piece grew more jovial as Elise continued to empty her purse. Gold fell upon silver, which made a bed for notes. Now bankrupt, she turned the purse towards him, to which the busker flashed a smile through his self made maelstrom.

The last notes of his serenade ended, and he began the ritual of packing up for the day. First, he scooped his takings from the case. Then he brushed the dust of resin from the strings and body with a soft cloth and the tenderness of a parent wiping their child's face. The chinrest removed, he replaced the violin. He eased the tension of the bow and slid it in a soft slip case. Elise watched him lay the chinrest and bow next to the violin and close the lid.

"Why no shoes?" she ventured. "Can't you find any that fit?" "You could say that." His voice sounded as lively as his notes.

"You know, I was just going to buy lunch," Elise said, "but I spent all my money."

"I know a place not far from here."

Elise soon found herself sitting opposite Peter, as he had introduced himself, over burgers in the Myers Centre eatery.

"So what do you do?" he asked.

"I'm a personal assistant at a law firm." It sounded less demeaning and more important than secretary. Even now, with her head filled with thoughts of how tonight might end, the shrill, broken-glass ring of her work phone intruded, along with the doorbell sound effect on her computer that signified a new email.

"I'll let you in on a secret," he leaned across the table, close enough to warm the blood in her veins. "I work as a waiter, but I'm really a violinist. What did you want to be as a child?"

She took the lid off her coke and stirred it with her straw. A few bubbles escaped to the surface and broke. "Promise you won't laugh?"

He nodded.

"Well, when I was about five, we used to have this cat. I just thought it was so unfair that he didn't have to go to school, and got to play all night. So I vowed to be a cat when I grew up."

"You were more imaginative than me then. I always wanted to be the fifth ninja turtle."

"But . . . " Each heartbeat was beginning to feel like a shoal of fish swimming through the chambers of her heart.

"I'm not a fighter."

He had given her only half of the famous expression, shy of an admission as lover. Elise tried to coax the other half from his lips, almost as perfect as his hands.

"So what does that make you then?"

"What are you doing after work tomorrow?" he countered. "It's just that I have to go make coffees for a few hours. But I'll be in the same place tomorrow."

She watched Peter fold his burger wrapper into an origami crane. With a small smile, he placed the crane on his empty cup and walked away, violin in hand. Café au Crane, such a waste of those hands, she thought. For a while, Elise pictured his hands transformed over time by his art. The finger tips of the left hand were heavily calloused, maybe with a slightly metallic scent, the right hand soft, but no less skilled. Tomorrow, she would see him again.

For once, Elise's lightheartedness back at the office was real. The usual making coffees for superiors and other ingrates (just another thing she had in common with Peter) didn't singe her with frustration the way it usually did. In fact, it was almost fun as she engaged with others about overcrowded buses and email jokes. The city even looked different through the office window, a steel grey all round where buildings seemed to have no end, and the sky no beginning.

As Elise pushed through the mall, she listened for a lonely violin amongst the rushing commuters and music from evening traders. She sustained a firm elbow to the shoulder from a businesswoman who yelled through immaculate red lips into a mobile phone as she looked elsewhere through silver rimmed spectacles. She looks like a stupid fish, Elise thought and giggled to herself. She walked towards the Wintergarden and he was there.

In an instant the notes captivated her and drove everything else away. He laid eyes on her and silenced the bow mid-stroke.

"So what's the plan?" she asked.

"You get to see my room." He took her hand before she could protest. Elise noticed the bright green nail polish from the office Christmas party. Ugh, I should have cleaned that off, she thought. Peter's calloused fingertips tickled her palm and the thought left her. Instead, she imagined those same fingertips brushing her nape, as they walked down Albert Street together and turned into Elizabeth Street.

Peter turned up a narrow staircase next to Elizabeth Arcade. Elise gripped the railing hard as she followed him. By the top of the first flight all she could hear was the echo of their shoes. By the second landing, she guessed she was out of screaming range too.

Above the stairwell hung a spider-web clad bulb. She thought of news stories of bad places and worse people. What if Peter was some darling of the underworld? Certain death could be awaiting her, for all she knew. She took a mental inventory of possible weapons in her handbag. It netted spray deodorant and a nail file.

"How much further is it?" she asked.

"Just one more flight." Peter turned around. "I guess they could use a lift in here."

Elise felt her shoulders relax a little at this joke, and her breathing became freer. But there was something she didn't quite trust in him, as though his shadow had detached itself from his feet to stalk her from behind. She gave a backwards glance, and by the time she looked forwards he was gone. True to his word, the stairs had ended and he was partway into the hallway that followed.

“It’s the door on the right at the end,” he said. “There’s a Hare Krishna restaurant on the left.”

Elise allowed herself to be ushered through the door. The room seemed to defy the length and height of the hall twice over, its depth likewise. It was only the obvious shop fixtures, a counter with an archaic cash register, a staffroom, and velvet curtained change rooms that grounded it in reality. The rest of its features gave the impression of the ruins of a ship’s hull run aground in the side of the building.

Vast and unpolished, the floor had a slight slope in the opposite direction of the street. All the windows hung open and askew in their casements. A giant mural of Tennyson’s Lady of Shallot was painted on the wall. There were oddly placed conveniences as if they’d been thrown about by a collision. In the middle of the floor was a sheetless mattress amid a few crates that served as seating. A rusty fridge hummed loudly in the corner. The room itself even smelled as though it had been holding some rare cargo with its scent of incense and damp. Elise was torn between horror and wonder at the room before her bladder called for a baser reaction.

“I need to use the bathroom.”

Under Peter’s direction, she walked down the short staircase behind the counter. The shop counter doubled as a kitchen bench and wardrobe, its shelves stacked with a minimum of clothing and crockery. She passed it and went through the beaded curtain. There was a bathroom stall, a corner shower with a curtain rail only, and a stainless steel sink. Most women would be disgusted, she thought, but Peter’s minimalist approach to living was beginning to appeal to her.

She opened the toilet door, and all thought was erased at the sight inside. A mural of the Queen Street Mall in oils occupied all walls, painted such that the sitter would appear to be standing at the lower end of the mall near Edward Street. The toilet itself was an anticlimax: a cracked, yellowed seat, although the cistern contained the vanishing point from which the rest of the scene to spread. Still unable to tear her eyes from the walls, she blindly shut the door behind her and slid the bolt across.

On the back of the door the artist had portrayed what could only be some kind of doom befalling the city. Where George Street ought to have been there was an expanse of sky reaching to the ceiling, occupied by some giant creature that appeared to be part bird, with rainbow feathers falling from its wings and tail like a hail of comets on the city.

On closer inspection, the picture was not as apocalyptic as it seemed. Above the toilet roll, which was affixed to the now demolished Queen Street Central building on her right, she saw where one of the comets had hit. Rather than destroyed, the building was changed.

She could see the faint outline of a door leading out to a balcony, and she was sure that the building had never sported a balcony in its day. Other buildings had sketchings of upper levels and new windows, as though they too had been growing under the strange rain.

As she stood to leave, she took one last look at the creature's eyes. They looked familiar, set in that inhuman face that held as much serenity as an eastern deity. There was no mirror above the sink, so she ran a brush through her salon-dyed hair and peered at her face in her compact mirror. Her mascara was slightly clogged and she pawed at it. Who am I kidding? A guy like Peter wouldn't care if I wore no makeup at all.

"I'm ready to go now," she called. Her words echoed back at her. "Peter?"

She drew the beads aside and peered out. The door to the apartment was closed, and Peter was nowhere to be seen.

Elise called his name twice more. A scrabbling from the ceiling, too loud to be rats or possums, coaxed her gaze upward.

Oh, how Peter had changed. From his toes sprouted claws; his skin gave way to feathers; and his bones had stretched and bent to form wings. The transformation failed Peter's face, its shrunken ears and pinched nose the only features that realised birdhood. Wings outstretched, he leapt from one of the rafters and flapped madly in a circle around the room. He came to rest on the floor in the back corner, his claws scraping the boards, wings beating against the walls. Elise watched him grip the curtain rail of one of the change stalls with his beak. He hoisted himself up and made a perch of it. Then he took flight again.

Elise edged towards the door, unblinking. Above her, a cobalt feather drifted downwards. The smell overpowered even the heady incense in the room. I'm not imagining this, she thought. The feather reminded her of a blue budgie she had owned as a child. His name had also been Peter, Elise thought as she plucked the feather from the air. She inhaled the familiar scent and remembered how Peter the budgie's warm body thrummed to his heartbeat as he sat in the palm of her hand.

"Elise, let me try and explain."

He began to walk towards her now, the lilt of his gait reflected in the creaking boards. She covered her eyes with the feather like a mask. To listen is enough for me, she thought. Through the blue, Elise could make out his impossible movement: his legs bent at inhuman angles. His head in sway from the birdlike stance was too much.

Somewhere in the midst of her flight, she thought of those Cluedo cards with the character's heads atop a coloured bowling pin shaped body. On the stairs, she realised how the Lady of Shallot must have been rendered. He needed neither ladder, hand nor brush. Maestro Peter had done it all with his bare wings.

A trail of saxophone notes from a blind busker in the subway corridor tore through her deadlocked mind as Elise ran to Central Station. Through the crush of commuters, she tore a stocking on the stair as the train doors sealed behind her. The city shut out, she found a seat next to a woman reader. That way she won't start a conversation, or worse, try to pick me up.

She looked past the woman and at her reflection in the window. Her hair was blown about like a shattered ghost, and she could see the whites of her eyes. For the rest of the way home she studied the other commuters.

Two men in suit jackets and ties, with recent haircuts and neat shaves, discussing the price of housing in outer suburbs, a youngish man in high visibility clothes listening to an MP3 player with a small esky on his lap, two schoolgirls giggling and peering down at their phones.

I will never be like them again, she thought to herself. For the first night in many months, Elise dreamed.

She became a child again, as she stood with her mother at the threshold of Hardgrave Park in the inner city. A mammoth striped tent filled the clearing, within it a force which buffeted the walls and ripped the pegs out of the ground and flailing into the silver moonlight.

Elise's mother gripped her hand and their eyes met. "Are you looking forward to the Circus Fantastique?" Her mother spoke with apprehension and excitement, as though she greeted her daughter after her first day of school.

Elise squeezed her mother's hand. "Don't worry, Mum."

The flaps of the tent rose open by an unseen hand, and the ringmaster came out. It was Peter. His feathers sprouted out of his collar, curtailed by a well placed top hat. Behind him, a blind busker with the body of a polar bear followed, bearing a leashed Labrador in one hand and a saxophone in the other. Elise recognized him from the mall and subway in the city.

A few other creatures followed with the heads of city buskers, the latter ones frozen in motion and drifting like anemones in an invisible sea. None of them were restrained, nor did they try to attack her, although they were close enough for her to prove them real.

Peter broke her out of her wonderment. He snatched Elise in his talons and rose into the air. Her mother's demands to have her returned grew more hysterical as they rose higher. Elise wanted to shout that she longed to join the circus. Peter's shirt and sleeves tore against his gigantic wingspan, and the fabric fell like snowflakes into Elise's mother's hands.

"Where are we going?" Elise asked.

"You want to join the circus, don't you?"

"Yes."

They burst through the roof of the tent and out over the cityscape. "Wow, it all looks so different from up here," she thought as they went over the matrix of lights from cars and buildings.

"Do you want to see the lions?" he asked her.

She nodded and they landed in King George Square. City Hall still housed the children's library and she would have longed for its books if not for the sights outside. The statues of lions were alive.

She patted their bronzed and furry backs when they advanced, harmless as hounds to their mistresses.

"In the day the lions are men," Peter said as he perched in a bottle tree. He had caught a worm and upturned his head to swallow it. "But tonight..."

Elise woke up in the early hours of the morning, those final words in her head and a maddening itch in her knuckles.

What did he mean? What would happen tonight?

She picked up the keepsake that proved her vision of Peter was real. Each strand of the feather was hard, sleek and straight. She closed her eyes and inhaled its aroma. The itching in her hands intensified, and a hunger swelled in her stomach. In her thoughts she saw Peter the budgie again, hopping from perch to perch and pecking at his mirror. It might have been an auspicious omen, had his tiny life not ended by the cat she had longed to be.

After work the next day, Elise stood outside Peter's room. All day her colleagues had whispered about the black dress she had worn to work. "Was she meeting a man?" they had asked.

"You could say that," she had replied with a coy smile.

She reached up to her ears and turned her earrings, and a memory of Peter the budgie ringing his bell with his beak flew into her mind. Her hands had itched all day, and she looked down at them. She still hadn't managed to remove that garish nail polish, and now her hands had broken out into a red spotty rash. Dermatitis and green, 'Merry Christmas,' she thought.

Too sore to knock, Elise listened through the door and heard scratching and thumping on the other side. Her heart lurched as she pictured Peter in his betrayal of humanity again. Music broke into her thoughts, and Elise realised he had only unpacked his violin.

The door was unlocked and for a while, Elise watched from the threshold as Peter played his apologies. He stood in the middle of the room, where he had flown only yesterday and looked up at her from a song that begged her to come in. His hospitality garb had been replaced with something a little more bohemian, loose pants and a shirt which would not look out of place at... The Circus Fantastique.

So forlorn, he looked like many others she had met in her art classes and sometimes felt a little too sorry for. Unlike Peter, they had been boys that nursed soul terrors, and mined their wounds in the hopes of finding gold or a sympathetic girl in the process. Only for Peter, it was his body and not his soul that was tormented.

She closed the door and walked down the stairs, her footsteps amplified by her stilettos, which she commanded with heel-toe precision. His eyes followed her every move. But wasn't it she who wanted to be a cat when she grew up? And did that not make him the bird?

"So, are you going to tell me what happened yesterday?" she asked

He put the violin down, the bow crossed over the bridge. "I didn't mean to change like that. I tried not to scare you." He walked towards her now, like an animal approaching its mistress for a scolding. Elise held him, for she knew she had seen his deepest secret, and it was something wonderful. "There are so many truths to tell," he whispered.

"Then I would like to hear them all."

"I'm not really a waiter."

"It's not often people tell lies to make themselves seem less impressive."

"I had to leave you on the first day because I thought I was going to become the bird." He gazed towards the window.

"What's it like?"

"At first, my heart feels like it is spreading wings, except one wants to fly east, and the other west. After this tug of war, my bones lighten and the feathers cut through, so seamlessly it's as though marrow becomes feather."

"That sounds painful." The image of Peter as a bird walking came back to mind. "Does it hurt to walk?"

"Yes. But it's very liberating to fly."

"I know."

"You dreamed of us then?"

She turned his face towards her and smiled. "Good. Shall we try going out again?"

"Maybe we should wait until dark."

"No. You'll just have to trust me until then."

Peter had chosen the perfect confessional at the Southbank war memorial. To Elise, the distance effected disembodiment on the city, a sea of silent buildings. On the southern side of the river Elise picked out a student, dressed in ragged pants and a homemade t-shirt which read "Critical Drinker". A group of serious cyclists rode by, dressed in bright lycra and chattering loudly like birds. Then there were groups of Japanese or Chinese tourists sharing a barbecue, their languages like song as they marvelled at and photographed attractions. Right now Elise felt just like one of them, seeing the city in a way she'd never seen it before.

"I call this the overworld," Peter said.

"What do you mean, overworld?"

"Each city has an overworld of artists and architects that create the city and change it all the time to capture the imagination of its people. From here, you can't see the people in the buildings and streets, only the buildings and streets themselves. Before they were constructed, somebody imagined them."

Elise stared up at the stone archway and silently read a plaque which revered the dead and wounded.

"You say you dreamed last night," Peter interjected.

"Yes," On her way to Peter's apartment, she had seen a security guard outside a bank, motionless as a statue. Thinking of her dream, she had tried little tricks to attract his attention, brushing her hair, checking through her purse, pretending to stub her toe. Their eyes had locked, and she saw what she wanted—a trace of the lion by night. "You said in the day they are men, but at night…" She turned and moved close enough to kiss him, but he pointed behind her.

"Look to the west, Elise."

Elise looked over to the Victoria Bridge where a small crowd of pedestrians had gathered. She pointed them out to Peter. "Look, even these people are gawking at us, waiting for us to put on a show."

"Then they'll talk about it for years to come. Hold onto my back. It's sundown."

She took hold, ear pressed to his back, and listened to his heart beating and almost tearing in his rib cage. The bones grew lither, and his outstretched arms seemed to bend to snapping points. Sleek and strong, feathers shredded his shirt. Elise's gaze was drawn to a crimson plumed shoulder, and further along to an elongated bicep, concealed by vermillion feathers. She tightened her grip on his shoulders. Beneath her nails, she felt trapped feathers.

Peter's body stiffened and he turned his head 180 degrees to face her. Elise saw little windows to pain and fear in his wide dark eyes, and he took flight towards the river.

Only when they had left the war memorial did Elise realise he could not carry her weight. He flipped like a kite in a high wind. A rain of feathers fell around her as she hung from his shoulders like a novice trapeze artist. She looked down at a crowd of upturned faces and palms, grasping for the rare plumage. Critical drinker was there, red faced and grinning. The tourists flashed their phones at her. Their shouts grew louder and more incoherent, their faces dull and grainy.

Oh no, Elise thought. I think I'm going to pass out.

Feathers came away in her hands, and the sea went skyward. Adrenaline came, white hot, and she clawed at the air. Her screams came as squalls. The faces of the crowd changed, and they ran.

I've changed too, she thought. As a large cat, she'd found her feet easily. By her tail and whiskers, she landed with perfect grace. Elise looked down at her pale paws, the claws still painted their Christmas green. Where's Peter? He had flown towards town, probably back to his apartment.

To her surprise running on four legs was easy to master, and she cleared Victoria Bridge faster than the buses. Her fellow pedestrians dodged left and right to evade her, some almost landing in the path of oncoming traffic, others tossing phones and parcels into the river. She crossed narrow streets in a single leap and dashed between traffic on George Street. Back on Peter's block, she slunk close to the wall until she found the sweet smelling staircase.

Partway up the stairs, she noticed her paws had left a trail of paint in their wake, a dark yellow with black tinges. Breathless and slowed to a crawl, she made her way along the hall to his door. She stood on her hindquarters and scratched down the length of the door. On the other side, a heartbeat hammered and wings flapped. Peter answered the door, his torso half bald and more feathers falling around him. They left spatters of paint on the floor, while other feathers needled their way back under his skin. Elise stood shivering as he wrapped his wings around her and pulled her inside.

"You're terrified," he said.

Elise nodded and looked down at her furry yellow body, protruding from around her now ridiculous little black dress. She finally understood why Peter wasn't wearing shoes on the first day, she had no idea where her own had gone. He led her across the room to the mattress, where she lay curled in a ball. Her tail touched her nose, and she stretched full length, hiding her front paws under the pillow.

"Can you play for me?" she asked.

He obliged, and Elise lay on the mattress and closed her eyes. As man and beast he was an artist, only the language changed from notes to paint in the transformation. In her mind's eye, the music caught up the feathers like leaves in a high wind, and she imagined nights of bestiary and art, where she would learn to embrace her newfound existence, and days of humanity where she would love.

Megan Tones is a research assistant by day and a writer by night. She lives in Brisbane with her husband and four puppies, and hopes to become a writer full time. A previous short story "Thirteen" was published in Issue nine of Ripples Magazine. *You can reach her at meganjtones@gmail.com.*

A Moment of Rapture with Jacqueline du Pré

by Julie Kerr

Her first note is a thunderbolt
Crashing above the forest of instruments.
She holds her cello close, and I sense
The power in her touch.
Her bow blows the strings
And lets each phrase
Ring over me,
Wave after wave.
Her fingers breeze
Up the fingerboard
Higher and higher.
Her music is fire,
Though I shiver as I listen.

Julie dedicated this poem to Jacqueline du Pré, whose brilliant career was cut short after she contracted multiple sclerosis at 28. A few months after the poem was written, du Pré died at 42. They published the poem in Julie's high school literary journal, but it has an even better story. Julie went with her cello teacher Lauren to a concert by cellist Lynn Harrell. He had purchased du Pré's 1673 Stradivarius cello after her death, and so Lauren gave him a copy of Julie's poem. He read it and put it into his cello case. Five years later, he was again playing in Seattle, and Lauren was talking to him, and asked him whether he remembered that poem. He whipped it out of his cello case, where he still kept it. So, her poem traveled all over the world with a Stradivarius, du Pré's cherished instrument.

Julie Kerr was born August 24, 1971. She had single ventricle and transposition of the major arteries, treated with a Fontan operation at age 12 and a Fontan revision at age 28. When she died in 2007 at age 35, she'd been happily married for seven years. With a PhD in mathematics, she was a very successful cryptanalyst for the NSA in La Jolla, California.

CHAPTER 9

HEART WARRIOR AUTHORS

By now, you might have read several essays, and have seen that everyone has a story. Maybe you are thinking about telling your own story? This chapter contains excerpts from books written by heart warriors and essays by authors. We include Tori Geiger's opening scene of her book From Vulnerable to Victorious, *which details a defining moment in her life. It's a strong start which I'm sure will leave you wanting more. Jessica Carmel shares her experience of gallbladder disease post-transplant in* The Hearts of a Girl. *In her story, she describes the pain she lived with for two years, and the uphill battle she and her mother faced to find doctors who would listen. A serendipitous conversation with a family friend steered them in the right direction, but they still had to convince the doctors. In the end, their tireless advocacy won out, and her story is a powerful lesson in not giving up.*

The other two essays in this chapter are by authors. Kimberly Russell's 'You Should Write a Book' (something many of us have probably heard) is about why telling our story matters. Feeling dubious at first, she soon found that sharing her story helped others in the CHD community, especially parents. Her involvement in the Adult Congenital Heart Association and encouragement from others inspired her to write a memoir, In a Heartbeat: A Child's Heart, A Surgeon's Hands, A Life Of Miracles. *Brandon Lane Phillips, author of* When I Wished Upon a Star, *met child actor Jeremy Miller from* Growing Pains *via a Starlight Children's Foundation gift, and the two formed a special bond. His essay 'Full Circle' talks about the impact of that encounter on his life, his journey to medical school and beyond with a learning disability, and his experiences since writing his book.*

I have yet to write a book but have found getting my own stories on paper (so to speak) daunting, be they fiction or reality. Like many people, I have the modern-day equivalent of partially written manuscripts shoved in drawers—files and folders all over my computer full of snippets of ideas, lines I love but don't have a home for, and so many beginnings. If you're like me (or even if you're not), I hope this chapter encourages you to write those first words.

Excerpt from:
From Vulnerable to Victorious

by Tori Geiger

Chapter 1

The crowd was roaring, and the gym lights penetrated the game atmosphere. It was a fierce game against the Blanchet Cavaliers, and we had been preparing all week for this game. As a freshman in rotation on both the JV and varsity teams, there was nothing like a big game in the rival's gym.

After finishing up the JV game just minutes before, I rushed over to the main gym to join the rest of the varsity in warm-ups. I had just had the game of a lifetime during that JV game: seven three-pointers, 30 points. It was one for the record books, and I was soaring high. So was my heart. The nerves of this game and excitement of the previous one were an overwhelming feeling.

Cheering on my varsity teammates from the bench, standing and sitting constantly, the game intensified with every bucket and shot. Ba boom. Ba boom. Ba boom. Ba boom. I can still hear it in my head. My heart was racing. But I was fine, I told myself. I got this. I wanted to get in the game and get my varsity minutes in, especially coming off such a hot streak at the JV Game. Then the gym started spinning. This wasn't good.

I grabbed our team trainer. "Ty, something doesn't feel right. My heart is pounding uncontrollably." He laid me down behind the bench on the gym floor and continued to take my pulse. You could see my heart pulsating out of my chest at this point. It was a riveting scene. My whole body was shaking from the effects of the fast-paced rhythm. It wasn't slowing down. I couldn't catch my breath. This couldn't be happening.

"We better call an ambulance," I heard Ty say to my dad and his training assistants. My vision was going in and out at this point, and the next thing I remember I was being rolled onto a stretcher with many curious eyes around the gym watching intensely. The doors to the ambulance shut. My dad sat on one side, and the paramedic sat on the other side.

"This is only going to be a pinch," the paramedic said as he hooked me up to an IV. "Can you tell me your name? How old are you? Do you remember what happened? Are you experiencing any pain in your chest right now?"

So many questions.

"I … I … I …" It was so hard to breathe. "I am so out of breath. I can't really talk," I said as I tried to answer his questions. That must have been a trigger because the next thing I heard was, "Code Blue!"

— *From Vulnerable to Victorious: Turning Your Chronic Illness Into Your Victory Story* by Tori Geiger

Going into code blue that night in high school has been the most traumatic event I have ever experienced in my life to date, but it was also one of the most defining moments in my victory story. It was the catalyst that "shocked" me back into the reality of living with a congenital heart defect. One that reminded me that my true superpower comes from being vulnerable and sharing the journey with others. You know what? Laying on that cold gym floor during that traumatic night, I so badly wanted to pretend that I was a "normal athlete," not an athlete with CHD, but that just wasn't my story.

After that night, it was through sharing the hard times, the battles, and the scars that I experienced healing in my own journey, and through the years, my CHD has taught me that true strength and courage come from being vulnerable. That's where true impact can happen too, and that's what I strive for each and every day. Through the journey of sharing my story with others, I have been building my resilience muscle, stronger and stronger. That muscle formed from my CHD experience has become the superpower that has allowed me to achieve more dreams as an author, life coach, and business owner than I ever thought possible. Even though it was terrifying at the moment, that code blue launched me into a purposeful life that I am so grateful to lead today.

Tori Joy Geiger was born in 1997. Tori lives in the wine country area of Newberg, Oregon. She is a passionate entrepreneur and has owned multiple businesses serving a variety of needs from the time she graduated college in 2019.

Tori has undergone multiple open-heart surgeries and procedures throughout her life. Growing up, she was an avid athlete, participating in volleyball, basketball, and track in high school. She played volleyball at Corban University and later joined the track team at George Fox University as a high jumper.

Part of her mission is to have a "heart that beats for others," and to help others achieve the same. Tori does this through her 50/50 CHD Promise; 50% of her blogging commissions are donated to CHD organizations.

Abridged Excerpt from:
The Hearts of a Girl

by Jessica Carmel

CHAPTER 16
Brave

"Maybe one of these days you can let the light in
show me how big your brave is
Say what you wanna say and let the words fall out"
–Sara Bareilles

"Doctor shopping" is a curious phrase, especially when it's used in a derogatory way. Why wouldn't you try to find a doctor who was going to listen to you and help you find answers to why, after a heart transplant, things weren't getting better? Dr. P had accused us, well Mom, of doctor shopping. It basically means that you, the patient, have several doctors that you are requesting care from, with none of the doctors knowing about each other. Sometimes people addicted to painkillers do this. They go see several doctors to get multiple prescriptions. Each doctor believes they are the only doctor that the patient is seeing and more than willing to prescribe painkillers or whatever the patient is requesting to treat the ailment.

I couldn't understand why Dr. P would (think) that this is what we were doing. For one, they were the one and only transplant team we were seeing. I didn't even know of any other transplant doctors. Because no one was helping us any further with my stomach problems, we were clear about wanting a second opinion. It is every patient's right to get a second opinion in order to find a doctor with whom they feel comfortable and believe they can trust. It is not a simple task to find even one doctor who would take on such a complicated case, let alone a handful of them. I was not looking for prescription drugs from any of the doctors and my mom wasn't either! The pain in my side and back went right through me, taking my breath away. My mom insisted there was something more going on than gastroenteritis, so she pressed the doctors to figure it out.

Then Mom had one of those lightbulb moments during a conversation with a close friend of the family. The friend told her that her granddaughter, who also had multiple heart problems, had had her gallbladder removed at seven years of age because it was causing problems. She explained her gallbladder had shriveled, and the family was told that there was a connection between congenital heart disease and gallbladder problems. It was a long shot to even suggest it to the cardiologist, but everything my mom had read and researched seemed to make my symptoms a little clearer and point to something possibly being wrong with my gallbladder.

I went in to Dr. P's office for an emergency appointment a few weeks later. I saw the transplant nurse practitioner, Meg, who had known me for a long time before she worked with the transplant team. She had been a nurse on the cardiology floor, and I always asked if they could put me on her rotations when she was working. She was my favorite, and I knew she took great care of me. When I wasn't having a good day, she always made me smile when she came into my room. So I was beyond excited when she became one of the nurse practitioners for the transplant team. We knew each other well, and I thought she would be the one person who could help and who understood me.

Doubled over in pain, I told her about the newer symptoms of the piercing side and radiating back pain. I couldn't eat anything, especially greasy food and foods high in fat. My mom suggested that we have my gallbladder checked. She repeated what her friend had said about her granddaughter with CHD. Mom explained that she, herself, had had gallbladder problems, which suggested a possible genetic factor. Meg said, "There is no reason to. We know you have gastroenteritis and that probably is what is causing the other pain." My mom turned, looked at me, then turned back to Meg and told her she wanted it checked anyway.

We assumed that Meg and the rest of (the) heart transplant team knew that the immunosuppressive medications, Prograf and CellCept could cause gallbladder problems. Information about it was available on the Internet. To make sure for myself that I wasn't crazy, I did my research. I decided to Google, "Gallbladder problems after a heart transplant" and "gallstones and gallbladder disease symptoms." Sure enough, there was evidence that it was possible after transplant that the patient could develop gallstones, biliary pain or colic. The University of Maryland Medical Center webpage gave me the best description. Most symptoms listed were ones I had complained to the doctors about for months.

I clearly remember Meg telling my mom and me, as we waited to see Dr. P, the immunosuppressive medication could affect my gallbladder. It was reassuring to hear her tell us that, but I didn't understand why everyone was telling us it wasn't my gallbladder. That was the first of at least a half a dozen tests; ultrasounds, MRI's, x-rays, CT scans, stomach-emptying tests, blood and urine tests. Every single test was negative, but the symptoms were only getting worse. They remained that way for the next two years.

Dr. W was my regular cath lab doctor, the one I requested every time I needed one. I got to know him and his dry sense of humor well. We respected each other, and I trusted him, literally, with my life. Mom and I went in one afternoon to see if we could get the results for one of my tests for gallbladder issues from Meg. She explained nothing showed up on this test, much less any of the other tests that I had done. I will never forget it. I was with Mom standing just off to the right of her. Dr. W was behind the check-in desk when Meg was going through every detail of what the test showed–no sign of gallstones. Dr. W's look was, "You have got to be kidding me! You guys are back, and you keep making a big deal out of nothing. It is all in her head." My heart sank at the look on his face. As he walked away, he muttered to Meg and my mom, "It is probably just her menstrual cycle. It will go away eventually."

I just could not understand why they wouldn't help. So what if the test showed everything was normal? Something was clearly not normal. The doctors said that if the test came back negative, then there was nothing more they could do. Eventually, they tuned me out when they asked how I was feeling or if something hurt because my answer would be, "Yes, I don't feel good at all. The pain that is wrapping around to my back in unbearable. I can't eat, and I'm throwing up bile." I threw up bile when there was nothing left in my system to throw up. A common symptom of gallbladder disease is the inability to tolerate greasy foods. French fries, pizza, cheese, and pretty much any fried foods were bound to lead to an immediate attack. It helps in breaking down all the fats, and when the gallbladder is not functioning properly, it cannot process these fats and the bile works against the body because it has nowhere to go. I was told to try antacids to help with the acidity from the bile, which was normal. Normal? I don't think so. Many nights I would come down to Mom's office and tell her the pain was awful and I couldn't take it anymore. She didn't know what to do at this point and her only suggestion was to call the doctor on-call to see if he or she had any suggestions, at least for the pain. We had every test done to rule out gallbladder disease and, with each, we hoped something would show up to prove I was really in pain and my mom wasn't crazy for insinuating that there was a problem with my gallbladder.

I would stand in the doorway of Mom's office as I called the transplant doctor on call. The doctor would call me back an hour later telling (me) they looked over my chart, and all they could suggest was that we head down to the emergency room. Clearly that wasn't helpful, and I knew I would just get sent right back home with no more answers or help than I had gotten before. The last thing I remember trying to eat was green bean casserole. I took less than a fork-full before I ran to the bathroom sick and throwing up because the green bean casserole had touched my lips and instantly made me sick. It was close to Thanksgiving, and I had been living with this pain for nearly two years.

CHAPTER 17
Angel

"Spend all your time waiting for that second chance
It's easier to believe in this sweet madness
oh this glorious sadness that brings me to my knees"

–Sarah McLachlan

We had made little progress trying to get the gallbladder problem under control. My mom, the family, and I were convinced that it was the gallbladder, but the doctors thought otherwise. Dr. L diagnosed the eosinophilic gastroenteritis, and, with that, he turned his back on us. There was talk amongst the doctors that I was a "trouble" patient and that my mom was only there to cause more problems. My mom was on a serious mission of looking for a new gastroenterologist in the Chicago area and soon got the name of one. My mom had a friend whose co-worker's husband was a doctor. He recommended a gastroenterologist at a downtown Chicago hospital. Both she and her husband had high praise for this doctor and said that he could help us. My mom gave the new doctor's office a call and scheduled an appointment.

. . . My mom knew I couldn't survive much longer the way I was living. I really wasn't living. I was miserable, sick, and in pain constantly. We finally were on our way downtown for the appointment. It was my first experience with a doctor that was not in pediatrics. I graduated to the adult hospital world, yet somehow, it felt more like I was thrown into it. Dr. P. J. Kahrilas would see me and take me on as a patient, but he told us he was not promising anything. All he could do was to help the best he could. He said he had another patient he had treated with the same symptoms and all normal results on their many tests, just like me. He said he suggested they remove the gallbladder and the patient's symptoms subsided.

Hearing that, my mom and I both knew he would be the one to figure out what the problem was. Dr. Kahrilas had my records sent over from the pediatric hospital, but he decided that repeating the tests would be best. Dr. Kahrilas did an endoscopy, colonoscopy, echo of my gallbladder, (and) a stomach emptying study. Instead of being injected with a radioactive material through an IV line, I had to eat a breakfast of radioactive eggs! I was sitting in the lab where the test was going to be performed when I got a plate full of the eggs. The thought of eating was making me nauseous. It took me at (least) 30 minutes to eat the plate of eggs. Once I finished, we had to wait a short time so the eggs could digest. They turned me nearly upside down, and side-to-side to see how my digestive tract and gallbladder were passing the radioactive eggs. We would have the results within a week.

All the tests came back relatively normal. Dr. Kahrilas tried putting me on some prescription antacids (heartburn medication) to see if that would help with any of the symptoms. They didn't help to any great degree, but I did what he suggested. He told my mom and me, in all honesty, that the only way to know if it was the gallbladder was to remove it. While leaving that visit, he reassured me that, even though the tests were normal, removal wasn't completely out of the question. He said he wanted to do some research to see if he could get any information about my anti-rejection medications and a relationship to gallbladder disease. He called my house on a Saturday afternoon, explaining to me he had talked to a fellow doctor and explained my case, including the medications I was taking. This doctor informed Dr. Kahrilas that two out of three people who are immunosuppressed have gallbladder problems and the only way to see if that was causing the problem was to remove the gallbladder. CellCept has listed side effects that could cause problems with the gallbladder.

I saw Dr. Kahrilas towards the end of October and by December he referred me to a surgeon to schedule a cholecystectomy (gallbladder removal). So I wasn't crazy! Because it wasn't obvious and no tests came back conclusive of anything, it became an unimportant detail to Dr. P, her staff and Dr. L. With the reassuring, kind, honest, and willing-to-help attitude of Dr. Kahrilas, we decided it was time to move on. We were finding another transplant team that could better support my needs as I got older. It was going to be much more convenient having all of my doctors under one roof, making a one-stop trip to the hospital. Aimee, a friend and fellow transplant recipient I had met a few years before at the start of my transplant process, told us about Dr. Cotts. She had since left the children's hospital and the same transplant team I had had a few years earlier.

. . . My appointment with the surgeon who was going to be removing my gallbladder explained to us that there was a 50/50 chance that I would feel better once they removed it and I was willing to take that chance. He also said that two out of three patients that were immunosuppressed needed their gallbladders removed because of problems with the functioning of the organ that sometimes didn't show up on any tests. There was one catch. He said he would not schedule surgery until after he came back from his vacation. It was about a week before Christmas when we saw him, and of course I hoped he would remove my gallbladder the next day, but really, my mom and I hoped we could get it taken care of before the holidays. Unfortunately, the surgeon did not want to schedule the surgery before he left. He knew my mom wasn't happy that we had to wait until he got back from his vacation and he had made a note or mentioned to another doctor as we left that day, that I was going to end up in the emergency room when he was out of town.

Well, sure enough, I ended up in the emergency room—twice. I could not stop throwing up and now the pain stopped me in my tracks. It felt like overnight everything got worse, enough for me to end up in the ER again. They admitted me to the hospital, and I spent another holiday season looking out a hospital window. The doctors tried to control the nausea and pain the best they could and scheduled surgery. Just after the New Year, I had surgery for a laparoscopic gallbladder removal. Dr. Shapiro was the surgeon, since the one I was supposed to see was still on vacation. Dr. Shapiro was friendly and compassionate.

I only had three minor incisions where they inserted the laparoscope, removing the gallbladder through one of the three incisions . . . Dr. Shapiro was great. I remember him coming to see how I was doing the next day. He only smiled and said, "Glad I could help!" It was a 45 minute procedure; well for me it was two years and 45 minutes.

It was almost immediate. The pain dissipated overnight, and I woke up hungry—really hungry. Food sounded good again, and the thought of eating didn't make me want to throw up. The nauseous feeling was gone. It was surreal how fast the symptoms had left after they removed my gallbladder. A few weeks after the surgery, we got a copy of the pathology report. It stated that my gallbladder was not functioning properly. Though there were no signs of gallstones or lesions, its function had been compromised. An unexpected and surprising bonus of having my gallbladder removed was that my seemingly endless migraines almost completely went away.

It had taken me a long time to accept that I was not crazy and there truly was something wrong. I learned a valuable lesson through both the heart transplant and the two years fighting for my gallbladder to be taken out that the doctors aren't always right. I knew there was something wrong and my mom knew it, too. Our strong gut instincts were telling us to not stop fighting until someone listened. We could have stopped, but the result would not have been as desirable as just holding on and fighting a little longer. I guess the best way, the only way to get through it, is to go through it.

Jessica Carmel was born June 7, 1983, in Northbrook, Illinois with HLHS, double outlet right ventricle (DORV), mitral atresia, heart transplant and kidney transplant. Jessica had a series of three palliative surgeries, culminating in the Fontan. At 15, she went into congestive heart failure and needed a heart transplant. Ten years later, she was in complete kidney failure and needed a kidney transplant. Her generous sister was her living donor.

Jessica received her bachelor's degree from DePaul University in Business Management and Entrepreneurship and her master's from DePaul in Health Communication. She also wrote and published her memoir, The Hearts of a Girl, *in 2016. Jessica is a die-hard Chicago Cubs fan. She has always wanted to throw out the first pitch at a game. Jessica's dog, Rocco, won the best pet costume (complete with jersey, toy bat, and under eye smudges) as a Cubs player!*

You Should Write a Book

by Kimberly Russell

"Kim, you should write a book," my grandmother would tell me occasionally. But I never understood why my life would be interesting to anyone. From my point of view, I was no one special and lived a normal life in small-town America. I liked the idea of writing, but who would want to read about my middle-class family or my middle-class life? To me, I was just a normal kid.

Years passed while I pondered writing a book, and why my life would be important to others. In 2004, everything changed when my cardiologist told me about the Adult Congenital Heart Association (ACHA).

"Kim, the next Adult Congenital Conference is in Rochester. I think you should come," Dr. Warnes, my Mayo Clinic cardiologist, commented. "There will be sessions on several topics dealing with being an adult with CHD."

At that point, I had met only one CHDer (because my CHD cardiologist set me up on a blind date with another CHD patient). To think that other people with CHD were out there intrigued me, so my husband Tom and I agreed to find out what it was all about.

To prepare for the conference, I read many outstanding books about CHD. I learned so much more about the development of diagnoses and surgical treatments. One book, *King of Hearts*, by G. Wayne Miller, described the development of operations for CHD. Who would believe that a parent could be cross-circulated with a child so that their heart would pump the blood while the child's heart was stopped for repair? It included the story of the first successful cross-circulation story of a father who agreed to cross-circulation to save his son's life. It was an amazing story!

We arrived at the conference a bit early and helped with the final preparations, and met some of the group leaders. Everyone at the conference was so friendly and welcoming! During meals, attendees could sit wherever they chose, so we sat with different people to meet and greet. While visiting with our new friends at lunch, I mentioned the book *King of Hearts* to express how good it was, mentioning the story of the first successful cross-circulation. It was really the beginning of congenital heart surgery.

As I was talking to one gentleman, he pulled out his copy and said, "Yes, I have read it. I AM that little boy." Tears flooded my eyes as I realized how current "CHD history" really is. Incredible!

My husband and I went home very excited about the conference and our new friends. Who knew how much it would change the course of our lives? We volunteered for ACHA, and I even became a board member. We have attended every conference since, except the one during the Florida hurricane. At every conference, they provide great sessions about different CHD topics, such as pregnancy, exercise, defect-specific care, and much more. Mostly we have enjoyed visiting with people who could relate to my medical issues. So much encouragement! At the end of each conference, we shed tears. Not saying "Goodbye," we say, "See you next time," hoping to attend the next conference.

"What an amazing experience to meet so many others," my Emory cardiologist said. "You know, parents from the heart center at Children's Healthcare of Atlanta (CHOA) could use the same encouragement. Here is the phone number to contact them."

A couple months later, CHOA invited me to speak at their next parent meeting. Nervous as I was, the presentation went much better than I expected. Almost every mother stood in line, some of them in tears, to thank me for bringing them hope for their children. Bing! On the way home, I suddenly understood my grandmother's words, "You should write a book." Parents and families would appreciate reading the story of my middle-class family and my life with a CHD. The next day, I bought a notebook and pencil, drove to my doctor's appointment, checked in, and started writing.

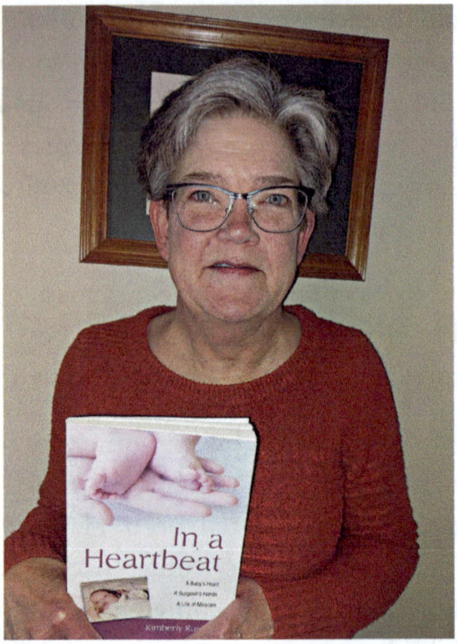

I wrote *In a Heartbeat: A Child's Heart, A Surgeon's Hands, A Life of Miracles* for parents, grandparents, friends, or anyone who has been affected by CHD. Because of the amount of research, it took two years to write. The story details were important. It was necessary for me to learn more about my surgeons and doctors through my surgical records.

During the process, I arranged a lunch with my first surgeon's wife. What a delight! The surprise and bewilderment on her face when she walked in was a joy and very emotional. "Are you Kim?"

I nodded while standing to greet her. "Yes," I replied.

"You're normal! You're healthy looking!" We hugged and tears slid down our cheeks. Meeting me reminded her that the sacrifices of being married to a surgeon were worth it.

To research my first surgeon, I went to Johns Hopkins. They have pictures of each class that Dr. Blalock taught how to perform the Blalock shunts. Looking up and down the walls, I didn't see a picture of my surgeon. An older gentleman came out of his office and asked if he could help. I explained why I was there, and he asked, "What was your surgeon's name?"

"Dr. Conrad Lam," I replied.

With his hands behind his back, he replied, "Oh, honey, you won't find his picture. He was brilliant. He heard about the surgery and taught himself." (I have a feeling it is good that my parents didn't know that.)

Apparently, he was extremely talented. I am one of his success stories.

Our journey has been full of challenges and successes. So many great experiences. After writing my book, they asked me to speak at events up and down the East Coast and a bit in the Midwest. My husband and I have met so many great CHD families and other adults who knew no one with a CHD or their specific defect.

My grandmother's encouragement to write a book has proven to be a great idea, after all. Helping others affected by CHD has been full of blessings for all of us!

Kimberly's book, In A Heartbeat, *reveals more about meeting and marrying her husband and the adoption of their two-day old daughter, Stephanie. Kim was born in 1960 and married Tom in 1981. They currently live in Atlanta, Georgia.*

They have spent several years advocating for congenital heart defects nationally and locally, including volunteering at Camp Braveheart for fifteen years. She loves her family and enjoys spending time with her precious grandchildren and great-grandchildren. (A podcast featuring an interview with Kim and her daughter Stephanie can be found at Lovingabrokenheart.wordpress.com, Episode 12.)

Full Circle

by Brandon Lane Phillips, MD

So many days feel surreal that I often wonder, 'Was it just a dream?'

As I sat in the makeup chair, I caught a reflection in the mirror of former child actor, Jeremy Miller, from that old 1980s TV show *Growing Pains.* He was sitting across from me. His face had aged, but he was still recognizable. Years ago, I liked the character he played on the sitcom and often wished that my home life was a little more like his fictional one.

"Close your eyes." The makeup artist powdered my face. "They are almost ready for you."

My heart raced as I walked onto the set of *Fox and Friends* with Jeremy to discuss our newly released book and our 30-year friendship. "Wow! This dream is wild! How did I go from my rural Louisiana life all the way to New York City to be broadcast across the nation?"

I called Dr. Tom Vargo in 2012 to share my good news. I had passed my pediatric cardiology boards with needed accommodations. It felt good to hear him call me "smarty pants." It was the highest I had scored on any national standardized medical examination.

Years earlier, I had experienced the same unbridled excitement that I had felt on the *Fox and Friends* set. I had been calm until Buzz Aldrin's name was mentioned overhead. I nervously began rehearsing my speech in my head. No one had told me an astronaut was going to be attending! Standing on the ballroom stage in the famous Beverly Hilton, I got a sense of déjà vu. I had certainly been here before, although not in this exact space. I saw many familiar faces as I glanced around the room. I knew some for the characters they had played in movies and television. A few had won medals during the Olympic games. And others were from the pages of history.

I stood there in disbelief as I shared the story of a young boy with a broken heart. I spoke of all the young lad's mother had done to make him less blue. In his eyes, his family had splintered because of his imperfections. I told how the work of the Starlight Children's Foundation had once brightened his world before presenting an award to the organization's chairman emeritus, thanking him for his dedication to children.

Many in attendance likely assumed the young boy was one of my patients. "Ladies and Gentlemen, please welcome Mr. Steven Spielberg," were the words that came out of my mouth, but the words that echoed in my head were 'Wow! This can't be real. I don't want to wake up.'

A few years before, I had walked across a stage in a New Orleans hotel to receive a scroll. "Dr. Brandon Lane Phillips," they announced. It was the first time I had heard those four words said aloud together. I had dreamed of this day many times before, but this version was better than the rest.

My long-time friend, Dr. Vargo, walked with me, placed a doctoral hood over my head, and exclaimed, "This is a great day, Doctor!" as we exited the stage. He had been there from the start and knew all the highs and lows that had led up to this day. At the end of the ceremony, my classmates and I danced down the aisle with green umbrellas in hand as a jazz band led our way out of the ballroom.

'Did that really just happen?' I thought as I remembered the countless times Mama had told me, "Don't get discouraged. God made up in your head what he missed in your heart." She tried to ease my self-doubt by encouraging my dreams, regardless of how improbable they seemed.

A few weeks before my graduation, I was having lunch with my friends when Dr. Vargo called to say, "Congratulations! I am so glad you matched with our pediatric residency program. I am going to help you find a new doctor, but I am looking forward to being your academic advisor during your time here."

I hung up the phone and rejoined Jeremy Miller and his co-star, Kirk Cameron. We were on the set of their second *Growing Pains* reunion movie, which was being filmed just up the road from my New Orleans apartment. They even gave me a small part in their film! I had dreamed of

(l-r) Kirk Cameron, Brandon, Jeremy Miller

reconnecting with the cast of my favorite sitcom many times. (More than once I dreamed the cast was on hand for the white coat ceremony that welcomed me into Tulane Medical School. Of course, they weren't there because that would be a little over the top. Sometimes my imagination could run wild!)

Growing Pains had been off the air for over a decade. Wasn't it unbelievable that Jeremy and Kirk were there to celebrate with me just as I was about to graduate from medical school and on the very day I would see my dream of working with Dr. Vargo come true? It all seemed unreal and yet perfect at the same time, especially since I began doing really well in school after I received my wish. I could barely wrap my head around all that had transpired in a single rotation of the Earth. 'A Hollywood writer couldn't have scripted it any better,' I thought as I drifted off to sleep. That was their last day of filming, and my friends left town the next day. Timing was everything!

During my third year in medical school, I was diagnosed with a reading learning disability. My internal medicine clerkship director insisted that I be tested after noticing that I did better on non-standardized exams. She knew that I had needed open-heart surgery following my first year of medical school. I was reluctant to be tested. I was already the student with the bad heart. I didn't want to be the one who needed additional time on exams, too. She was the first to tell me that learning disorders were common in people who had congenital heart defects.

When I was eleven, I needed another heart catheterization procedure. I was jittery and nervous, waiting for the procedure to begin. I begged Dr. Vargo to let me be awake so I could watch him work. He reluctantly agreed, but only after I told him, "I am going to be a cardiologist like you one day."

As I waited, I received a call from a lady named Amy who confirmed the Starlight Children's Foundation would grant my wish to meet Jeremy Miller after a month of recovery. "We've taken care of all the details. A limo will pick you and your family up at the Beverly Hilton. Jeremy will meet you when you arrive at the studio lot. You will have dinner with the cast, and Jeremy will give you a tour before you watch a taping of the show." Before I left the hospital, I remember thinking, "Did Amy really call?" The thought of that wish was certainly bigger than anything I could imagine.

They tested me for special education in kindergarten, and I continued to struggle with reading in the first grade. Having to repeat the year was devastating. It made me feel I wasn't smart.

Mama likely never dreamed her baby boy would be born with tetralogy of Fallot. How could she dream of something she had never heard of before my birth? I am quite sure my life today would be different if I had been born more normal. Growing up, I often wished my circumstances were different. Who wouldn't want to play football like their friends or have the perfect family like the ones you see on TV? Looking back, I realize I have been fortunate. My path in life has crossed with exceptional people, and some of them more than once. Many people don't live to see even one of their dreams come true. I have had more experiences and opportunities than I could have ever imagined. I have seen my life come full circle time and time again. Yet, at times,

I still wonder what life would be like without a heart defect, but deep down, I wouldn't want to change a thing.

The rest of my story can be found within the pages of *When I Wished Upon a Star*, a memoir penned with a childhood friend about the peaks and valleys of life.

Brandon Lane Phillips, M.D. was born in Alexandria, Louisiana in 1979. He was born with tetralogy of Fallot. Currently, he is a pediatric cardiologist practicing in West Monroe. He is best friends with an English Bulldog named Praline.

CHAPTER 10

BEYOND MY CHD

When a mother is told her child has a congenital heart defect, she fills her every waking moment with caring for, worrying about, and (for me) praying for that child. Occasionally, we moms allow ourselves a moment to envision our children as older, or dare we even say it—adults! To live beyond the congenital heart defect is a dream and the answer to countless prayers.

In this final chapter of our book, we have several essays by heart warriors who have dared to live beyond their congenital heart defect prognoses. These women, for indeed all the contributors to this chapter are women, are courageous and so determined. They have made every single day count, and they have learned important life lessons along the way.

We open this chapter with 'A Letter to My Younger Self' by Emily Falcon, where, with the benefit of hindsight, she gives her former self advice. In the middle, we have an inspiring essay by Michelle Anderson DeRoo, 'Exceeding Expectations,' which is one that I'm afraid far too many heart warriors will relate to. Initially, her parents were told she wouldn't survive to adulthood and later she was told her end was near, but those negative prognostications were wrong. Those doctors hadn't accounted for some things that medicine cannot measure nor quantify—courage, the desire to live, and sheer willpower. We conclude the chapter with an essay by Allison Holmes, who shares with us what she has learned after over 50 years of living with a single ventricle heart.

Medicine today has come a long way from the early days of pediatric cardiology, where most of the children didn't survive infancy or early childhood. We've also come a long way from the days of children being diagnosed as "cardiac cripples" and they were kept home from school to be taught by loving parents because schools were not equipped to handle children with special needs. We are so lucky to live in a time in history where now more adults are alive with CHD than there are babies being born each year. These essays would have been impossible to imagine by the parents of the authors. Megan and I couldn't imagine a better way to end our book.

A Letter to My Younger Self

by Emily Falcon

Dear Younger Self,

I want your life to be full of sparkle and happiness, but as a heart warrior, it's not always going to be like that, as it might be for other kids. As you get older and your heart health changes, your days may swing between crummy and livable. Glitter and fun will return, but you won't always be stable, and nothing will stay the same. Here is my advice from Future You:

What's special about you is not just your heart. Just because you were born in 1982 as the one out of every 300,000 people who have anomalous origin of the left coronary artery from the pulmonary artery, don't let it define you completely. Find the thing that makes you "you" and makes you feel strong. Be who you are.

Your body will forever betray you and will never be "perfect" or "healthy," but **there will be something positive to come out of every negative, even when you feel the most discouraged.** Yes, you will miss going on a big overseas trip, but when you recover from your second open-heart surgery, you will meet your favorite therapy dogs because you will qualify for a visit. Your fragility will vanish as you play together and you will be your old self, happy and becoming stronger.

Enjoy your appearance and hide what you want, but remember, bodies will always change. You don't have to love your body; you just have to tolerate it. Your scars will always be there, but you can accentuate whatever gives you confidence, like your smile.

Move past your fear of doctors; they want the best for you. Even though you'll feel like doctors are torturing you, doctors both familiar and new will do what is best for you, even if you don't always understand why. They will be your biggest ally when you need advice because they know you best. When you are thirty-one, the doctor you feared the most will come to your rescue and explain atrial fibrillation when you have it for the first time. He'll explain that you just need a tune-up like a car does to set your engine right again. Once you're treated, you'll be on your way out of the hospital like a car leaving a service garage.

People want to hug you because they love you, not always to monitor your health. Not every touch is someone counting your pulse or seeing if you're retaining fluid because of heart failure. Not every look is someone questioning why you are breathing like that, are pale, or have blue lips.

Be brave when it matters and advocate for yourself. Ask questions and fight for answers. You'll know something is wrong for many years in your early thirties and soldier on without a diagnosis. Keep complaining and keep questioning the doctors and you'll finally get the diagnosis that will improve your overall health.

Feel sad, angry, frustrated, happy and joyous when you need to. Chronic illness is a roller coaster and your feelings are valid.

If someone tosses you a ball, try to catch it. Run a mile at your own pace. **You'll never know what you can do if you don't try.** You'll join a softball team as an adult. You'll barely be able to hit a ball past the pitcher in the beginning, but by the final game, you'll score two points for your team and be the MVP (most valuable player) of the game.

Emily with mountain gorilla, Uganda: September 2022

Don't worry about what others think or say about your abilities. You're doing the best you can with your unique situation. Be proud of that. You're figuring it out. All that matters is that you're out there trying. Keep your head high. Everything you achieve is a win for you, your family, friends and doctors who don't care how fast you are, only that you are alive and well. Some people might be able to run a 5K in twenty minutes and it will take you thirty-eight minutes at your absolute best, but you'll get a finishers medal, just like them.

People will say stupid, hurtful things about your appearance and make assumptions about how you are feeling. **You'll meet people that say the wrong things throughout your life.** It's okay to be upset but don't dwell on it.

There's always someone else who is suffering too. Be kind. You don't know other people's stories, just as they don't know yours. **It's not always your turn to be the sickest.** Other people will someday experience some of the health trials you have been through.

Doing risky stuff can be a gamble worth taking. **You will remember what you didn't do, and regret what you didn't try.** For the first time in your life you will take a safety risk that isn't health-related and ride a motorcycle in Alaska. Yes, you'll almost fall off but those few minutes riding parallel to the sky and looking up at the sun you will feel the most alive, unafraid and proud of yourself for doing something scary.

Build a support system of people you can talk to about your true feelings and who can help when you are recovering from sickness. Find other heart warriors and share your stories, listen, and encourage each other.

Imagine things you want to do and achieve them however you can. Try to do something new, big or small, and don't feel discouraged if it doesn't work out. **Keep going. Consider what you really want out of life and do it.** You'll climb a glacier in Iceland and won't be able to keep up with the group, but a guide will take you up to the top at your own pace.

Appreciate whatever level of health you have. Some days you'll have strength and some days you won't. That's okay. Don't give up on yourself. Don't let anger concerning unfairness or illness consume you. **Why waste the time you have being unhappy?** Just because one day you can't walk ten minutes to the library, the next day you might be able to run two miles. Don't take what you can do for granted.

Find what gets you through scary doctor appointments and medical tests. You will write in your senior high school yearbook that sparkly shoes would get you through life, and you couldn't be more right. At age thirty-five when you meet your new cardiac surgeon for your second open-heart surgery, you'll wear your sparkly sandals and every time you're scared you'll look at the shine and feel better. Stock up on some sparkles for whatever the future holds. **Everything will be okay.**

Love,

Emily (1/2022)

Emily Falcon lives in Brookline, Massachusetts, born in 1982. At seven weeks old, she had a heart attack and was diagnosed with anomalous origin of the left coronary artery from the pulmonary artery (ALCAPA). This led to two open-heart surgeries, one at age six and another at age 35. She has a love for travel and animals, both of which have helped her get through difficult times. While living a constrained life, Emily has sought adventures whenever she can, such as volunteering with animals in Namibia, playing with wolves at the Arctic Circle, and eating with orangutans in Singapore. She is now an athlete who participates in a weekly run club and runs in 5K races throughout the year. She hopes to inspire others with health limitations to never waste a moment and not let life pass them by. Her memoir, From the Sidelines to the Finish Line *will be released in late 2023. Check out Baby Hearts Press for more information.*

Exceeding Expectations

by Michelle DeRoo

"There's nothing we can do. Some experimental trials are available, but you will need to relocate here, closer to the clinic. Otherwise, enjoy her while you can." As a child, my parents had been told that I was born with an inoperable heart defect known as truncus arteriosus. The prognosis indicated I would likely have a steady decline of health because of the extra burden on a misshaped heart and the corresponding impact on my lungs, which would cause my oxygen levels to be low and steadily decline with age. Not wanting to put me through experimental surgery, we went home. My life expectancy was 12–15 years of age, at best.

When it was time to start kindergarten, the local school district wanted me to be in a special school for disabled children. The logic was that with lower oxygen levels, I would have diminished learning abilities. "Certainly, you can see the burden having her in the regular class will cause the teacher. It will also be very stressful for the other students." This was not an argument the school would win, and I would not know about it for decades to come. My heart was special, but otherwise, life was the same for me as any other kid in the neighborhood.

As I entered my senior year of high school, we toured colleges and prepared for me to leave home on fresh adventures. My parents were nervous.

"Are you sure you want to go that far away? Maybe we should take a trip to the clinic and have a case review? Something to help you make good decisions living on your own?" We agreed that while I had enjoyed a childhood of relative normalcy, but without having to go to gym class, which made me the envy of every high school girl, it was sensible to see a cardiac specialist before I headed for campus.

Dad and I arrived at the clinic for three days of testing. Since they had seen me many years ago, comparisons could be made to prior tests and good decisions could be made. I had no recollection of my prior visit. Certainly, the tests differed from what my local doctor had run. We found waiting rooms the size of movie theaters, never-ending blood tests, and dozens, or hundreds, of people.

Tests started fairly easily, height, weight, chest x-rays, but the EKG (electrocardiogram) brought concerns. Dressed in a cotton robe, I lay down on a freezing table and they attached electrodes with wires to my body. Nearby exam rooms had patients busily coming and going, while they asked me to stay. Conversations started in whispers, but with added voices, they became louder just outside the door. Being cold and alone, a feeling of fear crept over me, wondering what the trouble was all about. They met my inquiries with, "They will discuss it in your consultation."

Pulmonology tests for lung function involved me climbing into a large plastic box where the only way to breathe was through a small tube. Slowly, breathing through the tube became harder and harder until I couldn't breathe at all. Soon, other clinic personnel joined to watch while they conducted the tests again. Being watched so closely, like a lab rat, only increased my anxiety. But again, the reply came, "They will discuss it in your consultation."

The echocardiogram was intense. The exam room was full of doctors, nurses, and students eager to see the test live. Being naked from the waist up and covered in freezing gel with an audience was terrifying. Midway through, additional observers arrived. It seemed to take forever. I cried through the whole test.

At last, the consultation day arrived. First, I met with a young cardiologist, Dr. Hurley, who was studying at the clinic. We walked through the test results.

"It's clear your body is struggling with the progression of your disease. It is best that you plan to come regularly for follow up. One of our senior cardiologists is going to speak to you regarding the ongoing planning." I was looking forward to hearing how to navigate the college days ahead. Surely, this doctor will have some good ideas on how to manage my illness in the future.

He was an older man. With dark glasses, gray hair, and a rotund body, he sat across from me.

"I remember seeing you as a child," he began in a gruff voice. "To be honest, I'm surprised you have made it this far. We don't see many patients with your physiology reach your age. Looking at my chart, he continued, "Based on your chart, you should be dead already."

Anger swelled in me, wondering how he could say this, but I kept my emotions steady. I retorted, "Well, I am alive. I disagree with you and obviously, God does too, or I wouldn't be here."

He continued, "I see the progression of your disease has developed into a severe case of pulmonary hypertension."

Trying to steer the conversation back to my college planning, I asked, "So, what does that mean for me? How do we manage my heart and lungs while I'm away at school?"

He looked at me with a stern face. "I don't think you are listening. You cannot go to college; you will not live to graduate. Go home and be with your family. The end of your life is coming soon."

Tears swelled in my eyes. "Can I see my dad now?"

"Good girl. Glad you are understanding what I am telling you." The senior cardiologist smirked.

In the waiting area, I fell into my father's arms. He calmed me down and asked the nurse if he could meet with the younger cardiologist assigned to my case, Dr. Hurley.

"Is it really the recommendation that she sit at home and wait to die?" my father asked the cardiologist. "How can anyone possibly know what her future holds? Shouldn't she be allowed to try?"

"Together, we can work a plan. She will need to be here regularly to oversee her progress and we will need to make sure her college is aware of her disease and has contact information should she need emergency treatment. I'm so sorry you had to go through this experience," Dr. Hurley said. We were told much later that they reprimanded him for contradicting the senior cardiologist, but he never wavered in his planning and support for me.

We all agreed that I didn't want follow-up care from the senior cardiologist who had been so defeating. Dr. Hurley would return to his practice in South Dakota soon, and a new cardiologist was starting at the clinic. She was arriving in the coming months from England and would take over my follow-up care from my next visit. I met Dr. Carole Warnes on my next visit. She has been an incredible force for good in my life. Helping me to make prudent choices while still enjoying life to the fullest. In the fall of 1987, I went off to college.

My college years were tough. Walking across campus was difficult, and the stairs in some of the older buildings without elevators were nearly impossible. These were the days before ADA (Americans with Disabilities Act) requirements, but over time, I learned to ask for accommodations when needed and would arrive to class extra early so I could rest prior to the beginning. Many times, it would be overwhelming, but I finished my freshman year with good grades and was accepted into the honors program.

In 1989, I had a stroke and my college days on campus ended. After brain surgery, rehabilitation and rest, I began again in night school while I worked during the day. Complex congenital heart disease needs medical insurance. These were the years when support programs had yet to be started. So, if you needed insurance, you had to have a job. The work/life balance was challenging, but I kept working on my bachelor's degree. It took 10 years to finish my bachelor's degree in finance.

In 2007, I completed my master's degree in business leadership. I graduated with a 4.0 GPA. My parents hosted a brunch for family and friends to celebrate.

I gave the toast, "Once upon a time, I was told that I wouldn't survive to graduate. That was 20 years ago. A big thank you to Dr. Hurley for having faith in me. My complete gratitude to Dr. Warnes for lifting me up and guiding me these many years. Thank you to everyone here for your love and support. Here's to another 20 years!"

My wonderful family has supported me in everything, and we have enjoyed many adventures along the way. I'm even a grandma! My beloved husband, Mark, tells people I am his hero. In truth, he is mine, supporting me in my life and career. He has always been there for me. I have had a wonderful career working in technology in the early days of the Internet. From working with the rocket scientists of NASA, to creating plans to place computer equipment in medivac helicopters, it has been a great experience that I enjoyed. Most of my colleagues over the years have never known of my medical situation. It is part of who I am, but not what defines me.

Sometimes, it crosses my mind that perhaps, if that senior cardiologist hadn't been so negative about my future, I might not have had the drive to achieve so many things in my life. There is no way to know for sure. I do know that the support of those along the way has helped me exceed my own expectations.

Michelle (Anderson) DeRoo was born in Elmhurst, Illinois in 1969. Sensing a heart murmur, her pediatrician recommended testing which resulted in a diagnosis of truncus arteriosus. At that time, surgical intervention was rare and with low survival rates. Her family chose to not go down the surgical path at that time. As a teenager, she re-engaged with the Adult Congenital Heart team at the Mayo Clinic where her condition has been managed without cardio-pulmonary surgery since 1987. Today she lives with her husband Mark and their dog Sophie in North Carolina. In 2016, she retired from a successful career in Information Technology and currently enjoys time with her family (especially her five year-old granddaughter) and friends, golf, and days at the beach.

Over 50 Years Living with a Single Ventricle: What I Have Learned

by Allison Holmes

Who am I?

My disability has shaped me, but it does not define me. It is a part of who I am, but it is not the core of who I am. I am much more than my limitations or my medical diagnosis.

My Voice Matters.

I must be my own best advocate by educating myself about my heart condition. The names and dates of my surgeries and procedures are now clear to me. When I don't understand my doctors, I talk to them, question them, and even change them if need be. When I was younger, I felt intimidated by doctors, but I don't feel that way now. I feel doctors are more comfortable and straightforward because of the confidence I display in communicating with them. I can only do this because I am knowledgeable about my condition.

Staying in Care . . .

I have learned the importance of staying in the care of a congenital cardiologist. They are specifically trained to work with CHD patients. Regular cardiologists are not very familiar with the structural defects we present and the comorbidities that may come along with CHD, such as pulmonary hypertension, etc. The importance of staying in congenital cardiac care was reinforced for me after being evaluated for heart and lung transplant, and they found a malignant tumor in my kidney. Because of the care I was receiving with my cardiac team, the cancer was found and successfully treated.

You can do it.

Living with congenital heart disease has taught me to be independent. From early childhood, I fought hard to prove myself, to be able to do things for myself and keep up with my siblings. Beginning at 18, I began taking myself to doctor appointments on my own.

You may need help sometimes.

Now, as I am aging, I am learning the importance of being open to relying on others when needed. As an older person with CHD, I realize I need more help to do certain things than I used to. There may have been times when I wasted more energy than I needed to because of my strong, independent nature.

You will live. Plan for it.

Live your life to the fullest of your capacity. Push yourself, but know your limits.

Make sure you plan for your life, i.e. school, career, health insurance.

I have come to the mindset that if you don't live a long life, it won't matter, but if you do, it definitely will make a difference in your quality of life. Don't worry about dying, just live your life. Worry is a thief and it will rob you of joy and happiness!

Dream.

Don't forget to dream. I have come to understand this late in my life. Because of the doctors telling Mom and me that my lifespan would be short, I didn't dare dream about a future until I became an adult. This is something that I still struggle with because it was ingrained deep into my psyche. However, I have been working on this. Last March I went parasailing over the Gulf Coast with one of my dear friends. It is a memory I won't soon forget and I look forward to going again.

There is Purpose.

There is meaning/purpose in what I am going through. It may take a lifetime to understand what the meaning or purpose is, but nothing happens without a purpose, not even CHD.

Be a helper.

Learn by what you go through and then help others with what you have learned. Once I discovered the Adult Congenital Heart Association, I knew I wanted to help others like myself. I became a peer mentor with the ACHA. It has been very satisfying for me, and I hope I have been helpful to those I've worked with.

I'm not the only one with problems.

My story is not unique. While I may have issues that no other may have, so many others have difficulties they struggle with too, medically or otherwise. I have encountered many struggling souls in my time. Everyone you meet is dealing with something.

The value of being understood.

People will never fully understand what you are going through. They are not you and they do not have your physical issues. You will need to learn how to communicate your needs effectively to your loved ones. Often, this is not easy. Be patient, but persistent. You don't have to be strong all the time. It is okay to show your weakness and give voice to your struggles.

Expect the unexpected.

Unexpected things will happen, good and bad. Health setbacks and/or cutting-edge medical technologies/treatments.

Not so fast!

It's okay to go slow or take a break; just do not stop and give up! Once when I went ziplining, because of the incline in the mountainous area, getting to the launchpad was quite challenging. But I slowly persisted, and I made it to the top! I was rewarded with an exhilarating flight through the forested mountainside.

Energy is gold.

Getting older with CHD, I realize my energy is limited. I feel I must guard it like it is gold! I need to set boundaries and learn to say "No" when necessary. My energy is valuable and I need to protect it.

Look for those who are like me.

Growing up with CHD, I never knew anyone like me. There were times of deep loneliness. The average person did not understand my specific situation, and it was frustrating. Once the Internet came to be, I began to look for people who could relate to my issues.

Even so, I didn't meet another heart patient until I was 45 years old. I found my Heart Sister in 2017 and our relationship has been such a blessing. I have also met entire communities devoted to supporting and advocating for congenital heart patients. If you don't have a local heart community, you can start your own! Talk to your heart clinic and share your information to see if you get any response. Then set up your own meet and greet, either in person or virtually.s

Don't lose hope!

Medical advancements are happening every day. I never thought that I would live 50 years or more, but thanks in part to the medical advancements I have.

Life is short.

It passes by in the blink of an eye. Don't put off the things you would like to try or experience. Enjoy them while you can.

Grow your Spirit.

This physical world and our physical issues are temporary, but our soul will live on after our body has expired. Do not neglect your soul. The joy of life comes from inside of us. What we nurture or neglect will impact every aspect of our life. For me, this means having a close relationship with Christ.

There is still much more to learn!

Allison Holmes was born in 1972 with a single ventricle heart. She has been with her husband Mark since 2000. She is a dog lover and dog mom to Duncan (Sheltie), and Ollie (Schnauzer) and an ESL tutor, teaching students who live in South Korea conversational English. Allison volunteers with the Meals on Wheels Organization and with Heart to Heart with Anna *in her free time. Allison is a Peer Mentor with the Adult Congenital Heart Association. Occasionally she volunteers with Carolina Waterfowl Rescue as a baby bird feeder. Allison believes in living the life she has been given to the fullest of her capacity. She is discovering the gift of giving herself grace. For Allison, it's not the quantity of life but the quality of life that she aims for these days.*

CONCLUSION

We hope you have enjoyed these essays from a remarkable group of people born with congenital heart defects. After four years of working on the book, talking to the contributors, using developmental editing techniques in order to help draw stories out of the contributors, and continuing to dig deeper for more meaning, I have learned that my heart warrior is right. These people are not "warriors" in the traditional meaning of the word. She's right in saying that the struggles and the fights that they must endure are simply for their own survival. However, having a book title like The Heart of an Adult Born with a Congenital Heart Defect just wasn't as catchy. Like it or not, the CHD community views these adults born with special hearts as "warriors" and I can appreciate their perspective as well.

During a philosophical discussion about the title of the book with my daughter, she mused aloud whether it was the parents who needed the label "heart warrior" to help them mentally in dealing with the arduous task of raising a child with a chronic illness. There is so much psychology that goes into raising any child. How do parents psych themselves into being ever-present in a world full of uncertainty, doctors, procedures, operations, negative prognoses, fear, anxiety, guilt, and pain? Do we need to view our children as "heart warriors" to give ourselves hope and courage? It's possible.

One thing is certain: amazing people created the essays, poems, and artwork in this book. Sadly, the word "amazing" is overused in today's vernacular. Dictionary.com defines the word "amazing" as "causing great surprise or sudden wonder." I think it is surprising that this cohort of people has survived, beating the odds and proving so many in the medical community wrong. How happy I imagine those self-same physicians would be to learn that science could indeed stay a step ahead of most of these contributors' needs. For many of the people, I think they would give a nod to the fact that God has had a hand in all of this, too. There are too many stories of people's experiences that qualify as miracles to deny a being more powerful than we mere mortals.

Thank God for the physicians, the nurses, techs, pharmacists, researchers, and scientists who have propelled the field of pediatric cardiology into the innovative discipline it is today. Thank God for the parents who never gave up on their children, allowed those same children to be the pioneers of a brand-new field of medicine, and who believed that their children could make it. Thank God for the people born with congenital heart defects who refused to give up, buckled down and created courage out of fear, and who came to realize that quality of life trumps quantity of life hands down. Thank God for the technology we have today that has let us render this book. Finally, thank God for you, dear Reader, for giving us a purpose in bringing these stories to light.

COLOPHON

Printer:

Lulu

Software:

Pages (for Mac)

Microsoft Word (for PC)

Template:

Free download by https://usedtotech.com: UTT-Books-39

Typesetting:

Pre-Front matter: Proxima Nova Medium, size 24

Front/back matter: Proxima Nova Medium, size 24

Byline: Adobe Garamond Pro, size 12, italicized

Volume divider: Proxima Nova Semibold, size 24,

kerning 50

Chapter titles: Proxima Nova Semibold, size 20

C60 M85 Y0 K0

Chapter dividers: Proxima Nova Semibold, size 20

Section dividers: Proxima Nova Semibold, kerning 50, size 24

First letter of chapter: Adobe Garamond Pro, size 35

Headers: Proxima Nova, size 8

Body text: Adobe Garamond Pro, size 12

Captions: Adobe Garamond Pro, size 8, italicized

The team:

Anna Jaworski, Megan Tones, and Amy M. Le were the developmental editors. Anna Jaworski and Megan Tones were also copy editors. Anna Jaworski and Lisa Colvil came up with the concept for the front cover, which was expertly designed by Omer Farooq thanks to Fiverr.

INDEX

You might also like . . .

Did you know that ONE contributor to *The Heart of a Heart Warrior* also wrote for *The Heart of a Heart Mother*? See if you can find out who contributed to both anthologies. If you read all the books in the series, you'll discover how some families have fared over the course of over two decades.

PRE-ORDER

20% discount: BHP20

babyheartspress.com

The Heart of a Mother Vol. One: Discovery

"I love this book, it is very powerful and heart warming. As a CHD patient I know first hand what my mother went through and for these mothers, it is amazing how they deal with this illness with their child and able to share their story." — L.C.

The Heart of a Father Vol. One: Determination

"So often in culture the "guy's" feelings are dismissed or overlooked...This becomes even more complex when working through the struggles associated with a child's chronic illness. The heart of a father takes a much needed look at just that, a father's heart."— J.M

20% discount: BHP20

babyheartspress.com

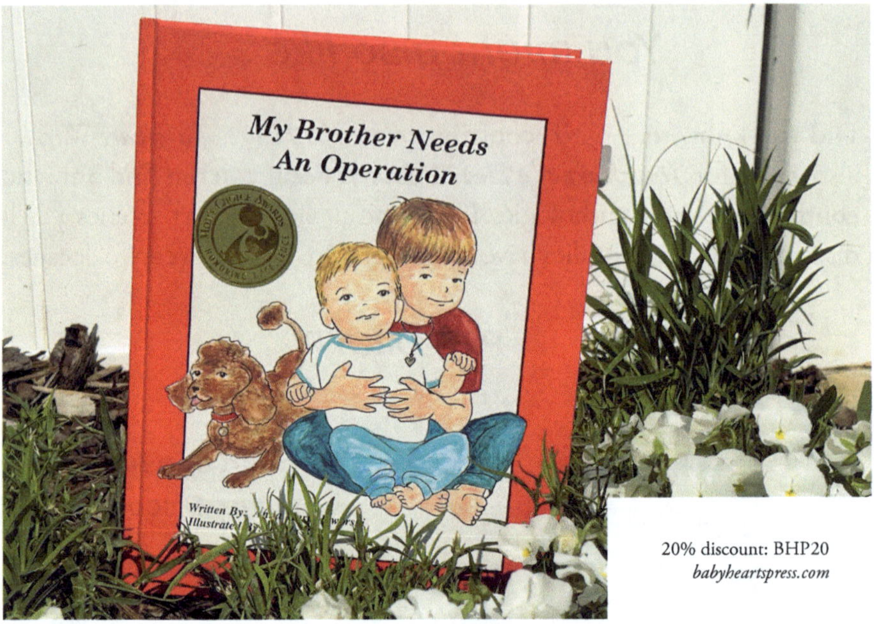

20% discount: BHP20
babyheartspress.com

My Brother Needs an Operation
by Anna Jaworski

"This book was recommended by a friend and it was an excellent investment for my children. Great interaction on each page to read to a younger sibling. Wonderful pictures that come alive...My 10-year old and 5-year old both loved this book. All hospitals should have this book on hand as well."— T

Did you know that "My Brother Needs as Operation" is a Mom's Choice Award winning book? One publisher even declared that the book was "an instant classic"! Do you have a child who will be left behind while your heart warrior is having surgery? If so, you need this book!

VOLUME ONE: SURVIVAL
The HEART of a HEART WARRIOR
Congenital Heart Defect Stories of Hope

VOLUME TWO: ENDURANCE
The HEART of a HEART WARRIOR
Congenital Heart Defect Stories of Hope

VOLUME 3: TRANSFORMATION
The HEART of a HEART WARRIOR
Congenital Heart Defect Stories of Hope